WARNING!

PROCEED WITH CAUTION.

Reading this book and experimenting with its 100 steps may change your life.

There may be no going back to the old you.

In other words, this is not another clever book meant to amuse you for a few minutes. Nor is it a guide for the dummies and inept among us.

But if you have ever wondered why it seems that a few people make all the difference in the world, and if you have ever wondered why some people seem happier and luckier than others—especially if you have ever wanted to be one of them—then this book is for you.

The premise is simple: all of us have the same access to God no matter what our particular beliefs may be. It is up to each of us to reach out and connect. Inside, you will find 100 ways to connect and all the reasons, too!

HOW to Get GOD on YOUR Side

100 Ways to Connect with God

Other Books
by Seymour Rossel

Alone and Wrestling: An Anthology

The Wise Folk of Chelm

Bible Dreams: The Spiritual Quest
*How the Dreams in the Bible
Speak to Us Today*

A Child's Bible (in 2 volumes)

HOW to Get GOD on YOUR Side

100 Ways to Connect with God

SEYMOUR ROSSEL

Rossel Books
Dallas, Texas

*H*ow to Get God on Your Side
100 Ways to Connect with God
Copyright © 2024 by **Seymour Rossel**

Thanks to **ClippyArt LLC** for selecting, adapting, editing, and at times entirely crafting the clipart-based illustrations.

Thanks to **Lorna Keating** for her nearly magical artistry in copyediting. She has a rare gift for making words shine.

Thanks to the remarkable **Kimberly Hitchens** and the excellent folks at **Booknook.biz**—they turn every publishing chore into a pleasure.

For further information contact:

Rossel Books
6523 Genstar Lane
Dallas, Texas 75252
https://RosselBooks.com

First Edition

ISBN:
978-0-940646-81-0 hardcover
978-0-940646-82-7 paperback
978-0-940646-83-4 epub
Library of Congress Control Number: 2023949699

Dedication

To **Michael (Mel) Glatzer**
and **Dennis Backer**
Nothing could be half
as wondrous or half
as mysterious without you.

Contents

HOW to Get GOD on YOUR Side

100 Ways to Connect with God

Introduction

Year in and year out, month after month, the old man prayed that he would win the lottery. He never did. After eighteen years, he cried out to God in despair, "When, O God, when will you answer my prayers? When will you make me a winner?" Thunder roared in the sky, and a lightning bolt struck the ground one foot from where the man stood. Then a voice boomed from Heaven, "When, old man, when? When will you buy a lottery ticket?"

It seems pretty obvious that you cannot win the lottery without buying a ticket, but it seems far less obvious to many folk that God will not answer a prayer that is never spoken. It seems pretty obvious that a lottery ticket always represents a potential win, but it seems far less obvious to many folk that getting God's help always depends on our potential.

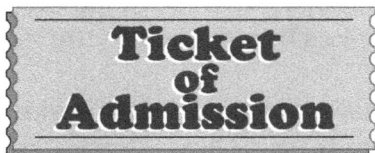

Ticket of Admission

It's no accident that this book attracted your attention. This book was written for you. Somehow you sensed that when you found it and again when you picked it up. You saw it on the cover. You heard it in the title. Now you are wondering just how this book will work for you. Can an author you have never met really have some personal message to deliver? The answer to the question is simple: Yes. If you are ready to buy the ticket.

You may be looking around at the world and noticing how other people seem happier or healthier or wealthier. Somehow, it seems, God must be helping them. If God is on their side, why shouldn't God be on your side, too?

You may be wondering whether highly paid executives or successful political leaders have some special connection that gives them their shortcuts to power and prestige. If it is power and prestige you are seeking, why shouldn't God be helping you to achieve them?

You may be listening to the latest popular singer or following the career of the latest television idol or movie superstar. Have they discovered a secret way of getting God's attention? Why should God be answering their calls instead of yours?

Or perhaps you think that some of these important and prestigious people have concluded a secret pact with the devil? Certainly it seems that those who purposely rise to do evil in the world manage to do evil without any second thoughts. It is inconceivable that they are in touch with God, for no God that we normally can conceive would condone such abuse of others. But it does appear that some power is helping them, at least for the time that they are successful. Maybe you wish that you could tap into their secret, too.

How can you get God on your side? How can you understand the success or failure of people all around you? Why do good things often come to evil people or bad things often happen to good people? What makes things happen the way they do in this world?

One thing is certain: the answer to this question does not depend on which religious faith you follow. Heroes and villains come from all sorts of religious backgrounds. The great who succeed and the simple who succeed belong to

each and every religious persuasion. No religion has ever
fully explained the success of the wicked or the suffering of
the righteous. Whether you are Catholic or Protestant, Jewish or Buddhist, agnostic or atheist, your odds of getting God
on your side in this world seem about the same. So the real
question is, "Is there a way of increasing your odds?"

That's what this book is all about, and that's why this
book was written for you. Will this be a book that changes
your life? It could be, but not if you ask, "When, O God, when
will you answer my prayers? When will you make me a winner?" Only if you are willing to pay the price to buy a ticket.

Getting God on your side has everything to do with the
ticket and the price you are willing to pay.

Welcome to
God's Place

I

Sneak Up on God

The preacher was greeting folk as they left church that morning when he spied a man he hardly ever saw. He took his hand and said, "We are so happy to see you and glad to welcome you back to the service of God."

The fellow smiled back and replied, "I am constantly in God's service, Reverend." Then he leaned close and whispered, "But I happen to be in God's secret service."

If we believe the statistics, most of us are like that fellow—part of God's secret service. About 50 percent of Americans haven't attended a religious service in the last

Poster Girl

God's Secret Service
FASHION DESIGN 007

three months. One out of every three of us has not been to a church or synagogue for at least a year, and those are averages, which means the number of people who go every week pretty much cancels out the number who never go, leaving the rest of us.

Of course, religion is not only—or even primarily—a matter of attendance at group prayer. Everyone knows that you can talk to God anywhere you please and at any moment you choose. In this sense, getting in touch with God is even more convenient than entering numbers on the touchpad of your cell phone.

But if you have been in God's secret service for a very long time—not reaching out and not calling out—God might be surprised to hear your voice. And there is a chance that your reaching out will actually produce results!

You might try sneaking up on God by doing the unexpected. Here are four simple ways of getting started:

1

*L*ook up at a tree and think about the fantastic design by which trees silently serve us—breathing in the gases (poisonous to us) that we breathe out; providing us shade, wood, sap, and so on—and give thanks to God for the miracle of trees.

2

Thank God for what you have—whether it is a little or a lot. Make a contribution to charity; it doesn't matter how much. In the case of most charities, a little goes a long way.

3

Make a phone call to help a friend in need (you can almost always find one if you think about it), and then thank God for choosing you to help.

4

Send flowers to someone you have not seen in a long time. Just enclose a note saying something like, "Thinking of you." Thank God for friends.

Okay, so you sneak up on God by doing something simple. How do you know that God hears you? Your first clue will be in the way that you feel about yourself. Do these kinds of things often, and your next clue may be in the way others feel about you. You may find it even more gratifying to be in God's service than in God's secret service.

Then the old axiom will be true for you: If you want what God wants, then what God wants will be what you want. Or as

Taking Sides

"Be on God's side and you can be sure that God is on your side."

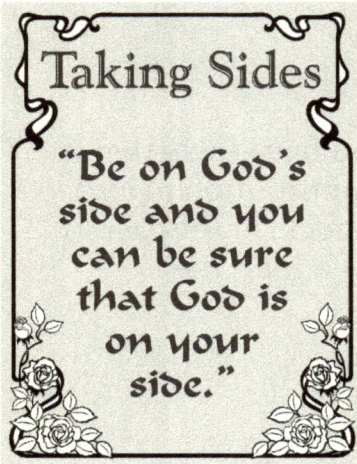

we may say it, "Be on God's side, and you can be sure that God is on your side."

II

Learn to See the Angels

The Bible puts a lot of stock in angels. When the prophet Elijah's life was in danger, God sent an angel to protect him (1 Kings 19:5-7). Daniel was protected by an angel in the lions' den (Daniel 6:22). Angels announced the birth of Jesus to the shepherds out in the fields surrounding Bethlehem (Luke 2:8-15). Peter was twice released from prison by the intervention of angels (Acts 5:19; 12:10). Most of us understand these as just Bible "stories"—ways the ancients had of expressing their innermost beliefs.

Except for occasionally seeing angels in movies and on television, or seeing them in books and on wrapping paper, our general impression is that if angels exist, they are unlikely to impinge on our everyday lives.

Wrong. You do not have to be a true believer to know that an-

JOIN THE BAND

gels are all around us working in the real secret service of God. In truth, we have no way of knowing how often we are directed onto the right path or protected from dangers by unseen forces. We can even learn to be angels ourselves.

One legend tells how the prophet Elijah continually wanders in this world, posing now as a stranger or even as a beggar. You could meet this beggar anywhere: sitting beneath the window of a bakery and too poor to buy bread; posing as a blind person on a street corner with just a few pencils in a tin cup; pretending to be a hobo or a member of the homeless sitting above a heating grate on a busy city sidewalk; or holding a sign that says, "I need work," at a traffic intersection. Any one of these people may be an angel in God's secret service.

You can:

5

Go into the bakery and buy a sandwich for the beggar outside. Thank God for the chance to be a holy consumer.

6

Buy a pencil from the tin cup of the blind beggar with a dollar bill and spend a minute talking with him or her. Human contact is just as important as the money. Thank God for your sight and for your insight.

7

When you are ordering a delicious restaurant meal, ask the waiter to pack up part of your meal to go and include a plastic knife and fork. Give that portion to the first homeless person you encounter. Thank God for giving you a meal you could share.

8

Keep some paper towels and glass cleaning solution in your car. When you see a person displaying a sign asking for work, pull over and ask for your windshield to be cleaned. When the windshield is clean and you have paid for the service, offer to leave the paper towels and cleaning solution behind. Thank God for giving you a chance to be of service.

9

Share your skills: Groups like Habitat for Humanity, food kitchens, and other community projects are great outlets for helping others directly. With so many families around the world in need, reaching out can provide great satisfaction. And what if you have no particular skills? Don't worry; almost anyone can make a sandwich or wave a paintbrush. You can thank God for even the smallest talent you have and bring it to play in the largest game of all, the sacred game of helping one another.

If encountering the poor is a test, you have passed it. In a sense, all of life is a test. Those who are homeless or forced to beg are human beings being severely tested. You are a human being required to reach out and help in order to pass your part of the same test. They are angels for you, giving you the chance to make yourself a better person. You are an angel for them, giving them a chance to get back on their feet and rebuild their lives.

Do angels really exist? You bet your life they do!

III

Give God a Chance

You are constantly busy. If you work away from home, you take work home. If you work at home, you keep working for hours after work should be set aside. If you are not working, you are answering e-mails on your computer or phone, watching television, listening to the news, shopping at the mall, driving to the grocery store, going to the movies, texting with a friend or a family member, preparing a meal, doing the dishes, helping a child with homework, making a scrapbook, practicing the piano, or playing a game. It never stops. Unless *you* stop it,

How can you know if God is on your side when you are too "busy" even to notice? Of course, "busy" is not bad. You can count yourself lucky to be busy. Many of us face other concerns when we are not "busy."

If we were to stop being busy, that might frighten us. We might suddenly feel ourselves becoming lazy, lonely, worried, anguished, grief-striken, sick, or dying. A lot of us feel that in the face of anything else, we should always keep busy. We should never allow ourselves too much time to think.

Well, what is the worst-case scenario here? Is it dying? Since death comes to all of us, it is a well-worn truth that we begin dying the instant that we are born. We may think we are lucky if we do not *know* that we are dying, but in essence this is just a way of fooling ourselves.

Or perhaps you do not mind dying so much as being lonely. Loneliness is a common ailment in our society. People may feel lonely even in the midst of a crowd, even when sitting with friends in a restaurant, even while chatting with family. Sadly, you may feel the loneliest even when you are not alone.

TAKE TIME OUT

Or perhaps your greatest fear is laziness. In a society such as ours that plainly prizes work, laziness becomes a stigma—so much so that many people work constantly just so that they will not have to face being accused of laziness. The person who never stops working is not necessarily exhibiting Type A behavior. He or she may just be running— running for fear that standing in place is an even worse behavior.

Yet the question remains: How can you know if God is on your side when you are too "busy" even to notice?

You might try this:

10

*S*top playing the game. Turn off the computer, put aside the scrapbook, set down the tablet, turn off the cell phone, and separate yourself from family and friends for a few minutes. Now, turn off the internal dialogue that tells you what to do and when to do it. Next, turn off the internal dialogue that buzzes with reminders of what is happening and what you should think about it. Take a deep breath and exhale slowly. And listen carefully to hear the sounds of nature. Don't stop breathing slowly, and don't stop listening until you get past everything else. Thank God for the miracle of silence.

If you receive a message while you are contemplating nothing, you may sense God's presence. But don't expect this to happen the very first time you try. You may have to repeat the exercise a dozen times or more before you feel something really important.

11

*I*n the middle of a busy day, make a conscious decision to stop what you are doing. Take a deep breath. Set everything aside and put your head down on your desk. Close your eyes, but stay alert. Close your ears to the sounds around you and listen for your own heartbeat. Thank God for the miracle of life.

12

In the middle of a meal, concentrate on tasting the food for its full flavor. Try to taste every ingredient. Let the food rest on your tongue just a little longer than usual. Thank God for the miracle of taste buds.

13

In the middle of a telephone conversation, take a deep breath and try to visualize the person to whom you are speaking. Thank God for the person who is reaching out to you. If it's a friend or a family member, hear their voice the way you first heard it, and thank God for your shared memories. If it is someone trying to sell you something over the telephone, try to imagine their life and needs. Think of the constant rejection they must face for just doing a job. Reach inside for a courteous way of saying, "No, thank you." Find a kind way of saying, "Goodbye and good luck." Thank God for giving you patience.

Of course, being patient or being quiet even for an instant doesn't come easily. Yet there are miracles everywhere

around us, each one crying out for our attention, but we can only give them due attention if we pause long enough to see, hear, and feel things in a deeper way. This all amounts to giving God a chance.

Answers We Sometimes Overlook

IV

Loose Change

There it is—on the sidewalk, on a carpet, in a hallway, in a train station, on a chair in the waiting room—a coin—a penny, a nickel, a dime, a quarter. You pick it up. You say to yourself, "A lucky coin!" You put it in your pocket and hope it brings luck.

Superstitious people sometimes say that a lucky coin is like a magnet, if you keep it with the rest of your change, it draws other coins to it. You chalk up this little piece of good luck to fate. But what is fate? Where does luck come from?

When luck is rotten, you know where to put the blame. You may say things like, "Everything is going to hell in a handbasket" or "I'm having a hell of a time." But when luck is good, you are more likely to say things like, "Fortune is smiling on me," or "I'm on a roll."

You find a lucky coin. It seems pretty improbable you'd think, "Wow! Just the other day I was asking God to help me pay my bills. I guess God is on my side after all. Thank you, God, for this lucky coin." But you may ask, "Is a lucky penny—even a lucky quarter—the answer to a prayer for financial help?" And the reply comes, "Just how much *would* be enough?"

There's a story about a little village that had its own local celebrity, a wise man who (so it was rumored) could work miracles. One year, there was a long drought, and the crops were failing. Finally, in desperation, the villagers came to the wise man and pleaded, "Make it rain so that our crops will grow."

The wise man shrugged and said, "The weather is not ours to control. Rain is in the hands of God."

But the villagers persisted, and finally the wise man said, "I will do what I can." The wise man climbed to the top of a hill and drew a circle around himself with his walking stick. "God," he said, "Your people are suffering, and they came to me for help. I will stand in the middle of this circle until You make it rain!"

A short time passed, and then a few raindrops fell inside the circle. The wise man looked expectantly at the sky, but no more rain was coming. "God," he said, "a few drops of water from the heavens is just a tease! I will stand in this circle until You make it really rain!"

Suddenly, clouds gathered overhead. Lightning scattered across the skies, and claps of thunder echoed through the valley. All at once, the clouds burst and rain fell in sheets. The wise man smiled and started to climb down the mountain satisfied that his prayer had been answered.

But he was not even halfway down the mountain when the villagers came running up to meet him. There was panic in their faces. "The rain is flooding the whole valley. If it continues, it will flood the village and wash away our homes. Hurry! You have to stop the rain."

So the wise man climbed again to the top of the hill and stood again in the middle of the circle. "God," he said, "I am standing here before You again. You must make the rain stop before it destroys us."

Just then the clouds divided, revealing the sun. The rain stopped, and the wise man left his circle again. And all the way down the mountain he smiled because he knew that he had become just a little wiser.

The lucky coin is like the first drop of rain. Whether you prayed for it or not, it came within your "circle." So you pick it up. But at that very moment, you are like the wise man before he learned the *whole* lesson God intended. If it rained like this constantly, you and everything you loved would be in mortal danger.

"To everything there is a season and a time for every purpose under heaven." That's the message for rain and the message for money, too. But a lucky coin can also be an opportunity for getting God on your side.

Consider how you could turn that lucky coin into something far more precious:

14

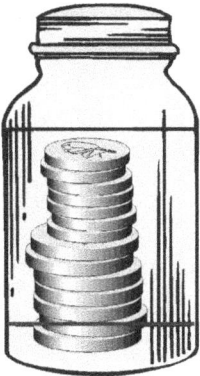

On the counter of the local deli or the local gas station there is a jar offering you a chance to donate some loose change to help children born with birth defects or chronic asthma or to some other fine cause. Thank God for your good health and put your lucky coin in the jar.

15

Keep a jar for "lucky coins" in your kitchen. Put every lucky coin you find in the jar, and ask everyone in the family to put any lucky coins they find in the jar, too. You might be surprised at how quickly the jar will fill—with coins found on the street, a little extra change that is too heavy for purse or pocket, a little change found in the living room couch that no one can truly claim, and so on. When the jar is full, meet with your family to decide what charity you want to support. Remember to mention God, for without God's help you wouldn't be able to have this family meeting, you wouldn't be among the fortunate people who can donate money to charity, you would-n't know where your good luck was coming from. Send that message clearly up to God—this is one way you know God is already on your side.

16

Think of every lucky coin you find as a re-minder that someone else has lost a bit of his or her fortune—somewhere, someone is less fortunate than you. Take your moment of good luck as a token and an opportunity to send a donation to a charity. Don't fret over the amount. Make out a check or tap out a few clicks for five dollars, ten dollars, or a hundred dollars. Think instead about the holiness you can feel in the little act of writing that check or inputting that donation.

17

Give a lucky coin to a casual acquaintance or someone you meet in passing. Mention that this coin has brought you luck and say that you hope it brings luck to him or her, too. Thank God for helping us make connections.

18

As you pass through a toll booth in your car or arrive at the window of the fast-food drive-thru, give the attendant some loose change to credit to the next car in line behind you. If you want, you can turn and smile. If not, you can just enjoy the feeling of having done something entirely unnecessary for someone you will probably never meet. And at the very least, you can be sure that God has smiled on that person.

Loose change is never an accident. It's always an opportunity. If you look at it this way, your change may change you.

V

Nuggets of Gold

> We are here on earth to do good to others.
> What the others are here for, I don't know.
> —W. H. Auden

In the New Testament Book of Matthew, the Golden Rule is taught by Jesus: "So in everything, do to others what you would have them do to you, for this sums up the Law and the Prophets." The same rule appears in the Book of Luke. In fact, almost every religion has arrived at this rule in one way or another.

In the ancient religion of Zoroastrianism, the rule is stated in the negative as, "Do not do unto others whatever is injurious to yourself." In the Old Testament, God commands, "Love your neighbor as you love yourself." And close to the time of Jesus, the Jewish sage Hillel said, "What is hateful to you, do not do to your neighbor. This is the whole Law; all the rest is commentary."

The prophet Mohammed said, "Not one of you truly believes until you wish for others what you wish for yourself." The Hindus say, "This is the sum of duty: do not do to others what would cause pain if done to you." And the rule of Tao states, "Regard your neighbor's gain as your own gain, and your neighbor's loss as your own loss."

It may not be surprising that religions always arrive at something like the Golden Rule. After all, no matter where or

when we live, we are all human souls and all very much alike. The most surprising thing is that we have decided to call it the "golden" rule.

Generally, when we think of gold, we think of that which divides us. Gold is a commodity and has an established price on the open market. Gold is what the rich have and the poor do not have. People rush to find it, people steal to obtain it, and sometimes people even kill for it. It seems difficult to imagine that it should be the name of a principle that is meant to make life better for all of us.

There is no doubt that "gold fever" is infectious. Legend says that King Midas once did a favor for the god Dionysus. In return, Dionysus granted him one wish. Midas wished for the ability to turn everything into gold with just a simple touch. At first, things went well. Midas went room by room through his palace changing every ordinary object into gold. Pretty soon, though, the king grew hungry and thirsty. Much to his dismay, he discovered that whatever he tried to eat turned to gold as soon as it came into contact with him. King Midas finally understood just how foolish his wish had been. Forthwith, he begged Dionysus to cure him of his golden touch. The god instructed Midas to bathe in the Pactolus River, and ever since it has been said you can always find a little gold dust in that riverbed.

Each of us has a little of Midas lurking inside—a desire to have everything we touch turn to gold. And each of us has an inkling that if that wish were ever to come true, the gold would be the seed of our own destruction. So why should the "golden" rule take its name from this precious metal? It might have been better to call it the "peaceful" rule or the "decent" rule or the "elegant" rule or even the "simple" rule.

In the final analysis, the rule is just a suggestion—and not a very specific suggestion at that. It only becomes "golden" only when *we* give it the value that we would otherwise give to gold. It is only "golden" when we live by it.

By saying it is the "golden" rule, we glimpse something that religions have traditionally taught: "When you practice this rule, God rewards you by turning everything you touch into gold"—not the gold that chokes you when you try to eat it, but the gold that fills your life with richness. In other words, practicing the Golden Rule always brings God to our side.

19

Bring a little harmony to your next business meeting. When two people are arguing and the debate heats up, raise your hand and point out the obvious; we all want the same thing, and, although there seems to be a conflict, in reality both positions have some merit. You don't need to suggest the solution; you just need to remind everyone that "we're in it together." Once reminded, often a compromise will present itself. You can thank God for being able to see the "gold" in both sides of the argument. After all, the whole point of the Golden Rule is learning to see things from others' points of view.

20

Think of your strengths. Maybe you are calm. Maybe you are clever. Maybe you are humorous. Maybe you are thoughtful. Maybe you are helpful. Find people in your life who could use a little of that particular gift you have. Share a little of your talent with them. Tell them about people in your life who helped you gain your strength. Give them some clues for growing stronger and thank God that you have some clues to give them.

21

You have probably been comforted by a friend when you were feeling down. Perhaps

it's your turn to "love your neighbor as yourself." If being comforted made you feel better, then you know it will make others feel better, too. Think of someone in your life who needs comfort. Make a video call, pay a visit, send a card, drop an e-mail. Thank God that you are able to reach out with love and touch a person's soul.

22

Or make a greater sacrifice: Do this for someone who annoys you, someone who has wronged you, or someone you don't care for most of the time. Reaching out to people you do not normally like carries an extra reward. It can break the ice in even the most frigid relationship. Thank God for our human capacity to turn the devil of enmity into the angel of friendship.

The Golden Rule is not golden because it has the touch of Midas. We call it "golden" because it bears God's greatest riches.

VI

Answers, Not Questions

When you reach out for God's help, you want answers, not questions. Often, when people don't get answers, they figure that God is not there, or at any rate is not interested in them. An Episcopal minister friend of mine likes to point out that God gave a lot of answers in advance, but people have been turning away from God for many centuries. Why should God rush to answer them now?

You probably feel that there is a grain of truth in what she is saying. Religion does have a lot of answers to the questions that people ask. But people today tend to be alienated by organized religion. Even those who believe in their religion may ride it like a bus—stepping on and paying the fare only when it happens to be going their way. To many, it seems that being "modern" means they have the right to pick and choose which doctrines to believe and which ones are not intended for *them*.

In other words, I want God to speak to me only when I seek God out. My religion should give me answers and not questions. My curiosity extends only as far as *my* concerns, the concerns of *my* family, the concerns of *my* friends, and hardly a whit farther. I need my own burning bush, my own special place where God and I can connect. When I ask a question, I should be answered the way Moses was answered: directly and responsively—my question followed by God's answer. I ask, and God explains. I don't want my connection to God to take place on a party line or in a group chat—in a church or a synagogue or a mosque—where just anyone can interrupt at any time and a dozen questions wait to be answered at once. Like a person-to-person call, I want to ask and be answered directly. But where do I find *my* burning bush?

This personal demand and the view of my minister friend are not so far apart, though. There is a sense in which God provided the answers in advance and a sense in which my particular questions deserve particular answers. There may be a middle ground, a meeting place between religion and self.

An ancient legend states that the burning bush had been burning since the beginning of time. According to the Bible, Moses said, "I must turn aside to look at this marvelous sight; why doesn't the bush burn up?" The next verse says, "When God saw that he had turned aside to look, God called to him out of the bush." It was just an insignificant bush, not a tree. Anyone would have noticed a burning tree, but Moses turned aside to notice a small thing, a bush, a detail of nature that fired his imagination and inspired his life.

We tend to look for God in the larger things. Why did God let this war happen? Why did God allow my friend to die of cancer? Why doesn't God speak to us out of the heavens? But Moses noticed a small thing and discovered God in it. I have to confess here: I believe that every bush is burning, every small detail is a place to meet God. Every blade of grass has an angel over it and that angel is urging it to grow. It is no accident that every tree grows by seeking the warm rays of the sun and reaching out for the precious water of the sky. The heavenly Gardener has ordained it this way.

Even the large and heavy questions find their answers in the details. Did this war bring death and suffering? Is it not time, then, for us to bring an end to war? Did this cancer bring death and suffering? Is it not time, then, for the best and brightest among us to seek a cure for cancer? Do the poor go hungry? Does the widow starve and her children grow thin? Is this not enough to tell us that we must take special care of the poor, the widowed, and the orphaned? Do we need prophets to berate us and inspire us when we have the answers before us every day in the details of our lives?

And still every answer is a question, and every question begins with "quest." Seeking the answer is always a personal task. The hero or heroine is the one who turns aside to look, the curious, the intrigued, the person who does not casually pass by but who stops and wonders—the one whose life becomes a quest. Organized religions have many purposes—some noble and some not so noble—but among the noblest is the question that every religion asks, "What quest has God chosen for you?"—for you, and only for you.

Only when you see the details do you receive your mission from God just as Moses received his. In that moment, you can hear God's voice directly. In that moment, God is speaking with you. In that moment, you come to realize that every bush is burning.

23

Ask yourself, What quest is my life on now? Where did it begin? How did I come to know that my quest went in this direction? Did I hear an inner voice telling me the path my life should follow? Did I enter into a covenant at that moment? Thank God for giving you notice, for setting your feet in a direction, for allowing you to begin the journey of a thousand miles with a single step.

24

If you have not found your quest, look around you. What troubles you most about the world? Are your people enslaved in some modern Egypt? Do you feel a deep-seated need to come to their rescue? Is your family in need? Does leaving for work each morning and bringing a paycheck home every week bring you a deep sense of satisfaction for their sake? Your quest may be as simple as lending a hand or as difficult as rescuing a dying person. Thank God for whatever talents you possess to aid you in the

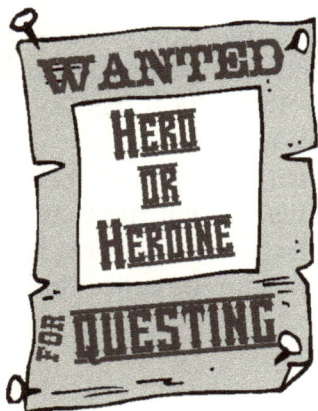

quest you choose for yourself and which you have been chosen to achieve.

25

Do you think you are not worthy of a great quest? Take the time to turn aside. What inspires you most? It may be something so simple and so ever-present that it seems obvious. It may be something that most people would hardly notice or that most would pass without any sense of wonder. Yet it is something wondrous to you—as wondrous as the bush was to Moses. Is it the sense of a special presence that you feel as you watch your kitten or your puppy grow into a loyal companion? Is it the

sense of a special presence as you watch a child discover what he or she will become as an adult? Is it the sense of a special presence as you watch the community in your church or synagogue grow stronger? Nothing flourishes without attention. Thank God for the opportunity to care for that which lives—not just for the ability to nourish it in body but also to nourish it in soul. Even the simplest quest may be a great mission.

26

Are you old, or are you young? The older we are, the more we realize that not every quest may be completed in a single lifetime. Many are destined to die in the wilderness, knowing where the Promised Land is but never quite reaching it. The young among us also reach out to the Promised Land believing they *can* achieve their goal, thinking nothing of mortality and seeing few limitations to their lives. In time, they also grow old. Yet there is nothing tragic in this process. We know that Moses never reached the Promised Land. He only scanned it from afar. The measure of your life is not necessarily in the tasks you complete but in the goals you set and the way you inspire others to continue moving toward theirs. Thank God for giving you life so that you could share it with others and not just in physical ways. When others see our path and know it is a good path, it inspires them to follow it, perhaps even to complete the work.

God answers many questions *with* questions and returns many inquiries with hints that lead us to quest for solutions. As you look around you day by day, keep in mind that every bush is burning. One of them burns just for you. Behind one of them, God waits to speak to you alone. Know that if you turn aside, if you are brave enough to take a second look at the details around you, you may be commanded to fill your life with meaning. If you truly want God to be on your side, you must truly expect to become God's messenger.

VII

Freedom Is an Answer

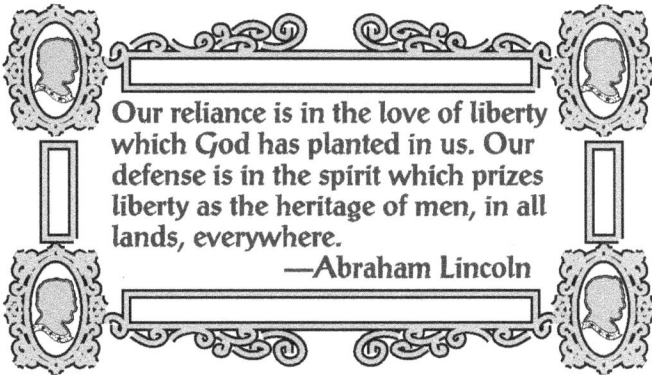

> Our reliance is in the love of liberty which God has planted in us. Our defense is in the spirit which prizes liberty as the heritage of men, in all lands, everywhere.
>
> —Abraham Lincoln

Our Founding Fathers were very much like us. At first, they were angry at "taxation without representation." Only later did they give wings to new ideals of human freedom. As Thomas Jefferson wrote:

> *We hold these truths to be self-evident, that all men are created equal, that they are endowed by their Creator with certain unalienable Rights, that among these are Life, Liberty and the pursuit of Happiness.*

You know these words—from school days, from political speeches, maybe even from church or synagogue. The ideas

were in circulation before Jefferson's time; they were hardly new, but in the Declaration of Independence they emerged as revolutionary.

Where do we get our rights? Neither from kings or queens or nobles, nor from some pecking order on a feudal chain. The Declaration said that our rights come directly from our Creator, from God. God is on the side of every human being. The Declaration singles out three of those rights as expressly being God's greatest gifts: "Life, Liberty, and the pursuit of Happiness."

God gives life, gives the right to exist. But by itself that is insufficient. Prisoners live. Slaves live. But what kind of life is that? Our Founding Fathers knew there had to be more. Hadn't God sent Moses back to Egypt to set the Children of Israel free, to remove them from slavery? Liberty, too, was a God-given right.

But now the Founding Fathers came to a sticking point. After all, death and suffering are part of life and liberty. No one can be happy all the time. We have no God-given right to be happy, but by God, we have the right to pursue happiness, to seek fulfillment, to hope for the best for family and friends. That right springs forth from almost every page of the Holy Bible, from Genesis to Revelations.

In honor of the Declaration of Independence, consider these possibilities for your own independence:

27

*T*ake a deep breath of free air. Thank God for the fact that you are living in a country that values your life and protects your existence.

28

*N*o matter what your job, contrast it with the kind of slavery that has haunted women and men throughout history. Under Hitler, slaves were worked to death in and out of the concentration camps. Under Stalin, nearly sixteen million people were sent to camps in the Gulag, enslaved for varying periods of time, many dying in servitude. In China today, slavery continues in the Laogai prisons, hellholes designed for physically, mentally, and spiritually crushing human beings. Thank God you live in a society that, for all its flaws, still treasures liberty.

29

*I*t's the weekend and you go shopping. It's a little spree. You may or may not find things to buy. You may or may not stop for a bite to eat. But you usually do not imagine yourself finding God at the mall or encountering the Divinity at the outlet center. Yet you are exercising one of those basic, unalienable rights—not the right to shop, but the right to pursue happiness. Thank God for the malls and the movies, the zoos and the playgrounds, the running tracks and the highways—for all the ways you pursue happiness in your everyday life. They are all proofs that God is on your side.

Still and all, there is a crack in the Liberty Bell. You are created with the unalienable rights to Life, Liberty and the pursuit of Happiness, but you know deep inside that these rights are constantly threatened and must be constantly defended. If you are in the armed services, it is because it is your turn to defend them. Police, firefighters, nurses, and emergency medical technicians— the uniformed services—are also defending our rights. Perhaps it is your friend, your child, or your parent who is on the front line of our defenses. Nonetheless, as we rediscover to our horror when terrorism strikes our nation or when our nation is forced to go to war in a very real way, all of us are on the front line always.

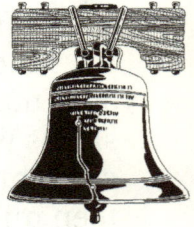

30

Thank God for those who step up to the plate to defend our rights. Take the time to smile at a nurse, a police officer, or a firefighter. Thank any soldier for placing himself or herself in harm's way. Give a friendly wave to the crossing guard. Tell an emergency medical technician you are grateful for his or her service. They are all guardians of life and of liberty; but for their efforts, there could be no real pursuit of happiness in our society.

31

No matter what age we reach, there are still people around us acting like nine-year-olds trying to prove how strong they are or how much influence they have by bullying someone weaker. Social bullies are not criminals. They usually bully others only if they think they can get away with it. Let a social bully *know* you are watching. Sometimes just a word or two help calm the situation. (Of course, it is far easier to alter our own behavior than to that of others, but it is always worth trying to help our weaker neighbors whenever we can. It brings a bit more peace into *our* lives.)

And remember that crack in the Liberty Bell. Like the Declaration of Independence, that bell is inscribed with an inspired verse: "Proclaim liberty throughout the Land..." Celebrate your life with all your being, cherish your liberty with all your heart, and pursue your happiness with all your might. Even if the Liberty Bell is now only a visual reminder of the mighty message it once rang out, *you* are free to proclaim liberty.

VIII

The Eyes of God

The much-revered teacher of Eastern religion, Paramahansa Yogananda, wrote:

The Lord is Spirit; the Impersonal is invisible. But when He created the physical world, He became God the Father. As soon as He assumed the role of Creator, He became personal. He became visible: this whole universe is the body of God.

Yogananda imagined that in the costume of earth, the north is God's positive side, and the south is God's negative side. He envisioned the grass and trees as God's hair and the rivers and streams as God's bloodstream. The heartbeat behind all heartbeats is God's, and behind the energy of the cosmos is God's energy. The sounds around us—the cries of infants, the songs of birds, the roar of waterfalls—are all God's voice. Even when you think it is God thinking through you, behind all the minds in the universe is God's mind. As the master teacher of Yoga said, "The stars are God's eyes."

Close to you, things seem to happen quickly. Though you know we have a history, things around you seem to be born, to live, and to pass away all too quickly. But when you look into the heaven filled with stars, what Yogananda called "the eyes of God," you may sense eternity.

For one thing, heavenly distances are so vast that we are forced to measure them in light-years. Light waves travel more than 9 trillion kilometers, or almost 6 trillion miles, in an earth year. It is 4.3 light-years to the closest star outside our solar system. That star, Proxima Centauri, is 25+ trillion miles away. In the heavens that is considered a short distance.

Consider an even larger phenomenon, the Milky Way, our own galaxy. We are at one edge of this galaxy and the other edge of it is about 100,000 light-years away—an astonishing 587 quadrillion miles. And the Milky Way contains more than 100 billion stars.

In the vast reaches of space, the Milky Way is not alone. It is part of a "neighborhood." Our nearest neighbors (only 200,000 light-years away) are the Large and Small Magellanic Clouds, small "satellites" of the Milky Way, containing only 30 billion or so stars. "Nearby," too, is the Andromeda galaxy (about two million light-years away and about the same size as the Milky Way). Our "neighborhood" in the universe contains two dozen or so galaxies. Astronomers call it "the Local Group."

If the stars are the eyes of God, then God has eyes everywhere: sparkling eyes, iridescent eyes, diamond eyes, luminescent eyes. And if the stars are the eyes of God, God has been watching for an enormously long time. It took more than four years for the light from the closest star to reach us, and millions of light years for the light of stars across our own galaxy to reach us.

When you look up at the night sky, you look into history. The lights in the sky are not the stars as they are today but as they were at the moment that the light set out to reach us—whether four years ago or two million years ago.

For example, Beta Centauri (the eleventh brightest star) is more than 300 light-years away. When you see its light, you are looking at what Beta Centauri looked like around the year 1700. What does Beta Centauri look like today? We will not know until some time after the year 2300!

Looking at the heavens reminds us that history is not something that we human beings invented. Like all the "facts" we possess, history is something that we discovered. As we spin around our star, the sun, we are little more than a tiny spaceship traveling through time. We are a speck in the universe, yet God has equipped our spaceship to meet our every need. As the visionary architect-philosopher R. Buckminster Fuller wrote:

> *We are blessed with technology that would be indescribable to our forefathers. We have the wherewithal, the know-it-all to feed everybody, clothe everybody, and give every human on Earth a chance.*

Realizing how small our world is, the French thinker Simone Weil wrote in her book, *Waiting for God*:

> *The children of God should not have any other country here below but the universe itself, with the totality of all the reasoning creatures it has ever contained, contains, or ever will contain. That is the native city to which we owe our love.*

From the heavens, it is clear that Spaceship Earth has no boundaries, no state lines, no national borders. Oceans connect continents. Skies are the atmosphere we share. The Internet did not suddenly bring us closer—long before the World Wide Web, we were a tiny speck spinning in the vastness of the heavens.

32

When something you are doing or something you are suffering seems endless, stand beneath the stars and look into history. What does "endless" mean in God's eyes? Some stars you see tonight no longer exist at all, yet their light shines on! If you do your best, surely your light will shine on after you are gone, too. Thank God for giving us this sign of the infinite light within us all.

33

Find a charity that does its work in a distant land. Make a donation—large or small. Perhaps you can feel how it is that oceans do not separate us and even space does not keep us apart. In God's cosmos all things are connected, all revolve around one another, all attract and balance one another. Thank God for enabling you to draw close to distant folk and to draw them closer to you.

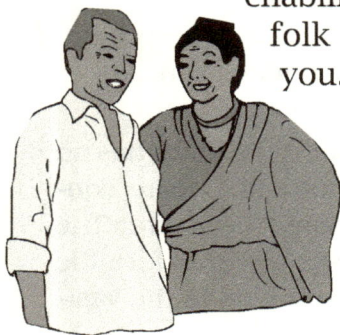

34

Become a star in your own galaxy. Drop a note to someone. It may be an old friend from college, a relative you have not spoken to for many years, a poet or author whose work has helped you or changed you, an artist whose works have moved you, a musician whose art has touched you deeply. Let someone know that you are thinking of them—that a bit of their light has reached you and lit up a bit of your personal heavens. And mention that you hope a bit of your light has reached them in return. Thank God for allowing us to light up the life of others and be lit by their light in return.

There is another secret in that sky at night; the heavens are really full of color. While most stars look blue-white to our naked eye, some stars are deep red while others are entirely blue or raging orange. In fact, the mixture of gases is different in each and every star, so each and every star is a slightly different color from every other. No doubt, somewhere in the cosmos, other beings are working and playing under the light of a purple sun or a crimson one.

35

Create your own sound and light show: The ancient Greeks believed that the heavens were filled with music, with each planet lend-

ing a note to the symphony of the universe. You can get a little of this mystical feeling by selecting some favorite music, turning off the lights, and sitting where you can watch the stars. Sharing this with family or friends might make it even better provided that you concentrate on the music of the universe until the music coming from the sound system fades away. After that, what you say to your partner or partners may be more intense, and you may all thank God for the spirituality built into the skies.

Is God on your side? The universe is one of the largest proofs of it. The conditions that make our life possible—a sufficient distance and closeness to the sun, a sufficient atmosphere to protect us, a sufficiently thin atmosphere to keep us from being smothered in gases, a sufficient distance to the next planet to keep us safe, a sufficient spin to give us gravity, and more—are all very delicately balanced. We may not be the only life in the vast reaches of the universe, but we are living proof of the genius of our Creator. That is another message reflected night after night in the stars, in "the eyes of God."

The Really Tough Questions

IX

Death and Life

Any book about getting help from God must deal with death, just as every human being must deal with it on a personal level. Life is never long enough. Even when a person dies of old age, there are those who would wish that he or she could have lingered a little longer with us, and the hurt and resentment may grow to staggering proportions when a child or young person is suddenly snatched from our midst.

Then, too, certain kinds of death involve suffering and may seem like cruel and unusual punishments. Deaths that result from accidents and natural disasters like floods, earthquakes, and hurricanes seem like aberrations—as if God were singling out people at random. And the deaths of those who are especially beloved tend to seem altogether unfair.

It is too easy just to say that no one likes death. If God is in charge of the universe as we believe, then life and death are both God's design. Can we honestly thank God for life and all its blessings even while we are cursing God for death and all its tragedies? Yet this is precisely what often happens. And the reason is not too difficult. When it comes to life, we may not have all the answers that we wish for, but life itself seems to hold answers for us. As long as there is life, there is time for things to change and reason to hope. Death, on the other hand, brings an end to time and hope.

Or does it?

Rabbi Maurice Lamm tells a story of twins waiting to be born. As embryos, they are warm and comfortable and well-fed. They have everything they need.

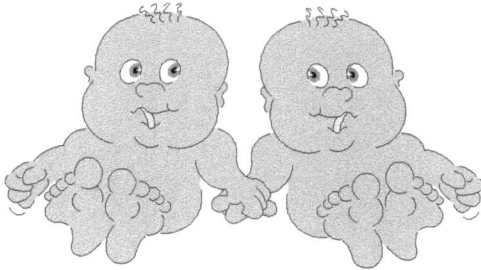

But one day they notice that they are moving lower and lower in the womb. What would happen if they slipped out? The first twin ponders, "Surely, there will be another life after this one." The second twin doubts this: legends about another life are nothing but fables.

The first twin thinks, "After this life we will see great things and taste new things and feel phenomenal emotions. We will be able to move from place to place and to hear wondrous sounds." The second twin thinks, "All these rumors are poppycock. It is your imagination running away with you. If you slip from here, you will die, and that will certainly be the end of you."

A great rumbling begins and turmoil ensues. There is a rush of liquid and then the first twin is slowly drawn outward from the womb. The second twin yells, "Stop! You are leading us to doom." But there is no stopping. The first twin disappears, and now the second twin is being drawn toward the same sad fate. The second twin thinks, "What a tragedy! Why should such a wonderful person be torn from our midst?" And just as the head of the second twin comes up against the opening, there comes the sound of a slap and a screaming cry. It is the voice of the first twin.

The second twin can only wriggle and twist, vainly resisting the opening. "Now, I must also go to my doom—to darkness and death, to oblivion. It is all just as I predicted."

That is how the story ends—and also how life begins. When it comes to death, it is up to each of us to decide whether we believe that it is the end of us or merely the portal to a new beginning, a next existence where we will perceive greater things, hear unimaginable sounds, and discover feelings we can only dimly comprehend.

Among the ancients, it was said that those who believed that death was the entry into a new life would find new life when they died; whereas, those who were convinced that there would be no life after death would find none. No one can assure us that this is how it works; no one can say the ancients were wrong. But the story of the twins in the womb gives us a clue to the mystery of life and death. And it is important to note that, the twin who believed in another life suffered less—even though both were destined to the same fate.

36

The light of a flickering flame has ever been a great metaphor for the flickering of life and death. Kindle a memorial candle for one you have loved and lost. Sit near the candle for a while and take in its message. Thank God for memory and meaning.

37

Visit the grave of someone you loved or someone you cared about. You might have a prayer in your heart that you want to offer, or you might bring along a poem to read aloud. Many find healing in reciting words at a grave site. Many sense a special closeness to a loved one there. Thank God for the quiet wisdom of the grave.

38

Graveyards are not just a final resting place for the departed. They are museums of life. Walk through a cemetery. Read the inscriptions on the stones. Consider the lives of those who are interred in this place. The human story unfolds as you pass from row to row. Thank God for our deep-seated need to remember and recall.

As it is written in the Book of Isaiah (57:1-2),

The righteous perish, and no one ponders it in the heart; the devout are taken away, and no one understands; the righteous are taken away to be spared from evil. Those who walk uprightly enter into peace; they find rest as they lie in death.

How can we enter into a life of righteousness so that we, too, may be spared evil? Only through repenting of any evil we may have done can this be. Reflect, then, on the sage advice to "repent one day before you die." Since we never know what day this may be, "repent one day before you die" can only mean that we must rethink our lives every day. It is by putting ourselves on God's side in this world that we truly prepare ourselves for the next world.

39

Thank God for the human capacity to repent and change, to dream and plan, to cherish and hope.

40

Turn off the television for one hour—there is usually an hour when nothing really appealing is on the tube—and write a page or two for your journal. Think of good things you have done or good things that have been done for you. Describe them briefly. Collect the pages. In times to come, your children and grandchildren, your best friend, your niece or nephew, will treasure these pages. They will be a part of the story of you—the meaning you found in your personal quest.

X

Suffering and Healing

All of us know that pain, at its core, is a good thing. It alerts us to the conditions of our bodies and sometimes even to the conditions of our souls. It awakens in us a desire to do something to cause pain to cease—to visit a doctor, to rest, to treat and bandage a wound, to take a pill, to change a habit. Without pain, we might neglect ourselves and deteriorate beyond the point of saving ourselves from ruin.

All the same, some pain is more a dreaded enemy than an annoying friend. This kind of pain is usually accompanied by its unkind partner, fear. As uncomfortable as the pain would be *without* fear, with it the pain is increased and the person who suffers may be driven to the edge of despair. Even in cases where the pain itself becomes little more than a dull ache, fear still intensifies the suffering.

Long-term pain is not only the fate of the dying. Many of us live with it regularly. We expect it in the case of various fevers and cancers, but we also find it in other chronic maladies such as debilitating back pain, arthritis, migraine headaches, stomach disorders, and skin disease—suffering with which we must learn to live. We may come to fear waking each morning to find that the pain has not disappeared but continues day by day. Eventually, we may fear standing or sitting, inhaling or exhaling, touching or being touched.

For all its advances, medical science can only go so far. Doctors and therapists can heal many of the causes of pain, but some pain can only be masked with drugs that may remove the physical sensations but do nothing to alleviate the fear. And at times the drugs themselves may cause a new kind of suffering—a senselessness or dulling of the mind that leaves us feeling helpless and hopeless.

Many who suffer turn to God only when pain cannot be treated by modern medicine. For quite a few, the operative question is, "Why me?" Why did God single me out to suffer? What did I do to deserve this suffering? Why should I suffer when others do not? All these are manifestations of the single cry, "Why me?"

But the facts are different when we stand back and look at life objectively. Pain was created along with us. It serves us. Even in the Garden of Eden, God reputedly put Adam into a deep sleep before removing a rib—the world's first operation and its first anesthetic to relieve pain. God knows about pain. God created pain. The pain that benefits us is the same pain that afflicts us. It is God's message.

It is only natural for us to turn to God in times of suffering, and it is natural that prayer should be a source of healing. We are not speaking of miracles here—though every evidence shows that miracles do occur and sometimes occur directly through prayer—we are speaking of the natural healing possible through sincere prayer.

Based on our belief in God, it is safe to assume that God hears our every prayer even though God does not always choose to respond. We are like children here, calling for our mother. She hears but does not think it necessary to come at that moment. Perhaps, she sends a friend or hands us a toy to keep us company thinking that will be enough. But when the child refuses to stop crying and continues demanding the presence of the mother, eventually she appears. "If you want to know God," says Yogananda, "you must be like the naughty baby who cries till the mother comes."

Make up your mind not to stop crying out to God. The Divine Presence will come to you if you persist. The Hindu scriptures say that you must talk to God with intense devotion for one day and one night. Then God will respond. Yogananda says,

But how few do it! Every day you have "important engagements"—the "devil" that keeps you away from God. The Lord will not come if you just say a little prayer and then start thinking of something else; or if you pray like this: "Heavenly Father, I am calling to You, but I am awfully sleepy. Amen."

Then, as Paul said in Thessalonians, "Pray without ceasing." God does not respond to the half-hearted. But let your prayer be as unceasing as the pain, and the pain may soon be overtaken, and the fear may soon depart with it. Or better yet, the fear may disappear, and the pain will become the more bearable.

And even this is not enough. To be alone in misery is debilitating. To have others around you who want to help is a comfort in itself. To have them join their prayers to yours may achieve a sooner victory over fear and pain.

41

If you are suffering, try to separate your pain from your fear. Determine which is causing you the most despair. Compose your prayer carefully, asking for what will be of most benefit. Thank God for your willpower and your faith, and send your prayer to heaven again and again.

42

You may be surprised to find the prayer resources all around you—in churches and synagogues, on the Internet, in small gatherings of prayer circles. As you pray for yourself, consider seeking out others who may also be in need of your prayers and joining with them in the work of prayer healing. Thank God for the blessing of companions, for our ability to share their needs and their ability to share ours.

43

Some of us feel unworthy of God's help, beneath God's concern, less than whole ourselves. Who are we to pray and ask for favors from the Creator? Then seek a companion, a priest or rabbi or minister, a devout friend, a person you feel is worthy. Ask for help in learning the prayers to say, the ways of expressing your needs, even for help in reciting your prayers and psalms. Thank God for those who already serve God that they may help us in understanding God's service.

44

*C*hoose a group or charity that deals with the kind of pain you are suffering and make a contribution to their work. Even if the cure does not appear in time for you to benefit, your making the effort to reach out on behalf of others may help alleviate your pain and bring you closer to working through your fear. Knowing that people are actively seeking a cure for what ails you is itself a great comfort. Thank God for those who choose to make their lives a source of healing.

45

*N*ext time you are at prayer—even if you yourself are suffering—pray for *all* suffering to cease. As it is said, "If you rise from your prayer a better person, your prayer has been answered." Thank God for allowing us this gift of inner spirit.

Long-term suffering—and also short-term suffering—may be built into the fabric of creation, but it need not be destructive. Like the kindest of all parents, God is always at our bedside.

XI

Proof of God

Every religion relies on faith. And we are often asked to test our faith—to find a way to believe despite what is happening to us or in spite of what our eyes sometimes see or our ears sometimes hear. "Keeping the faith" is not an easy thing to do.

Most religions find it necessary to plant a little fear in us to help us keep the faith. Preachers in old New England used to recite the horrors of Hell for hours on end to motivate their parishioners to adhere to the rules of their strict Puritan reli-

gion. This was, of course, close to what Dante Alighieri had done in the fourteenth century when he mapped the levels of Hell in his poem "The Inferno." The practice continues today. Generally speaking, in fact, all religions praise the fear of God in one way or another.

Fear alone is not enough to make a believer, though. Unless you first have *faith* in God, the *fear* of God is of little use. For this reason, religion is constantly called on to prove the existence of God. Religions do this in different ways. There are many Bibles—each a little different in their proof of God.

Some people read their Bible and accept its proof unequivocally. Some people read their Bible and find it less than persuasive. Even within a single Bible like the New Testament, different gospels contain different proofs and at times contradict one another. This is one reason that many people look directly to God for proof.

Gideon, who was destined to be a Judge of Israel, demanded proof of God's existence not once, but twice (Judges 6:36-40)! And Jesus responded to demands of proof by inviting us to, "Ask and it will be given to you; seek and you will find" (Luke 11:9).

The Reverend Billy Graham, knowing that you and I often want proof that God exists, put it this way:

What exactly are you expecting God to do? In other words, what would He have to do to convince you He was real, and that He loved you and would never abandon you? And how would you know it was God, and not just some trick of your imagination?

The answer to this question depends on each of us, for each of us is a little different and each of us has different needs. Do you need God to cure your illness in order to convince you that God exists? And if God cured your illness, would you know that it was God who did it and not the doctor or the therapist? Do you need God to speak to you directly? And if God spoke to you directly, would you know it was God speaking, or would you imagine that you were hearing voices in your head? Do you need God to protect you on the battlefield? And if you survive the battle, would you know it was God who protected you, or would you say that you were lucky that you survived? Do you need God to help you find a new job? And if you found a new job, would you know that it was God who helped you, or would you think that you found it by carefully following the classified ads?

Proofs of God can be confusing and confused. At the age of five, little Johnnie bent over a sheet of paper and began drawing with great concentration. Just then, his mother came into the room and smiled to see him so engrossed in his artwork. "What are you drawing, Johnnie?" she asked.

Without any hesitation, Johnnie answered, "It's a picture of God."

"But, Johnnie, nobody knows what God looks like," his mother said.

Johnnie replied, "They will as soon as I'm finished."

Lots of people throughout history have thought like little Johnnie. Their image of God was just what their personal vision of God was in every detail. Sometimes these kinds of pictures ended up in Bibles, but often they ended up bringing war and destruction. God was not to blame. Religion was not to blame. The "proof" was to blame, the "evidence" was to blame.

If you think you need to test God in order to know God, you will soon find yourself in the same predicament. Billy Graham avoids this by saying that the proof is in what God has already done.

You don't have to wait for God to prove Himself to you—because He already has! You see, the greatest proof that God loves us took place almost 2,000 years ago when Jesus Christ went to the cross for you and me. The Bible says, "This is love: not that we loved God, but that he loved us and sent his Son as an atoning sacrifice for our sins" (1 John 4:10).

The first-century Jewish teacher Akiba had much the same message for us:

We are beloved because we were created in God's image. Through superabundant love it was made known to us that we were created in God's image, as it is written: "For in God's image the human was made."

The only "proof" on which we can rely is the direct link between God and us, the existence of people who can perceive love and rely on faith, of people who can live and give to one another, who can fear God and turn that fear into good actions. You can test God in many ways, but the only "proof" is that you are here to make the test.

46

Help save the whales or help save the bald-headed eagles. Animal extinction is a problem exacerbated by human civilization. It is also a problem that civilization can solve. Keeping God's world intact is God-like work. Thank God for your ability to sustain the world's wonders.

47

Spend a full day greeting people with a smile. Don't distinguish between those you know and those you don't. Smile to everyone you meet for the entire day. Thank God for the infectious glory of smiles.

48

Contribute precious time to your community. Choose a committee in your house of worship or in other volunteer organizations. Volunteer for jobs that require actual effort. You will set an example for others. Thank God for our ability to help one another.

You can pass the test for God. As soon as you reach out your hand to another human being, as soon as you dedicate yourself to doing something that will alter the world for good, as soon as you devote your time and effort to making a difference, it is you who becomes a "proof "of God's existence.

49

*S*tudy the proofs of God all around us. Bless God if you are lucky enough to see a rainbow, to witness a birth, to hold your loved one close, to cuddle an infant, to change a diaper, to be awakened by the sunshine, to realize that a plant has grown toward the light, to identify the Big Dipper, or just to sit comfortably in a favorite chair or on a favorite couch. The more active you are as a witness, the more you yourself become a proof of God.

XII

Overcoming Despair

Every year, climbers come to Zermatt, Switzerland to test their skills against the peak known as the "Tiger of the Alps," the Matterhorn. They call the red sunrise on the Matterhorn's head, "a heavenly sight." As one climber wrote:

> I came to fulfill a childhood dream.... And what a view it is! Defying gravity! With its aggressive yet elegant looks! If you love nature, you must love the Matterhorn, the most beautiful mountain on earth!

From late September to early June, though, the pyramid-like top of the Matterhorn is often obscured by fog and cloud. The mountain vanishes into the hazy visage of the sky. This causes no confusion for the villagers of Zermatt. Even when its snow-clad top cannot be seen, they know that the

Matterhorn rises there in all its beauty, standing guard over them.

It is easy to feel the presence of God when we witness nature's wonders. Whether it is the indescribable glory of the Grand Canyon or the simple splendor of an open rose, we imagine that we see God's hand at work in the world. But the weather is not always so clear.

Shadows pass across every life. There are days of grief and despair, moments of sorrow and sad times. It is then that our hearts fill with the fog of doubt. The clarity we have about God's presence in moments of awe is transformed into a cloud of suspicion, the uncertain feeling that we have been abandoned. Unable to see the mountain's peak, we wonder if the mountain exists at all.

So it is precisely in times of distress that we require faith. When our lives seem rotten and spoiled like a vegetable long-forgotten in the very back of the refrigerator, when we feel like we should discard everything and just give up, that is when we need the certainty of the Zermatt villagers. The Matterhorn is there whether its head rears high in clear weather or is shrouded in the mists.

One of my friends is a nun who does a lot of work with drug addicts. She is a rock for them. And she often catches them off guard with her matter-of-fact spirituality. Listening to a narrative that would make most of us cringe, hearing of the horrors of a life descended into living hell, and knowing she has no simple answer to offer, she often responds by saying, "Let's take this one to God." All at once, without bowing her head or

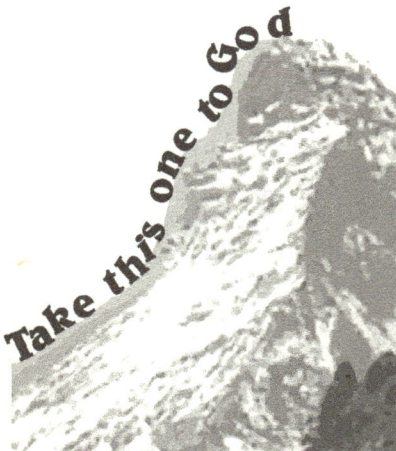

clasping her hands prayerfully, she addresses God out loud, asking God to answer the call of the needy soul.

Where did this open spirituality arise? As Sister Mary explains it, her aunt spoke to God constantly. Walking into a room and hearing her aunt talking, it seemed natural to think that her aunt was just entertaining company. No one thought that her aunt should be sent to an asylum. It was obvious that she and God were just exchanging views on the weather. It became just as natural for the niece to say, "Let's take this one to God."

How honestly and openly the Psalmist spoke to God in a moment of dejection!

Save me, O God; for the waters have come up to
*   my soul.*
I sink in deep mire, where there is no standing;
I have come into deep waters,
The flood sweeps over me.
I am weary of my crying; my throat is parched;
My eyes fail while I wait for my God.

When things are looking down, when you can't see your way ahead, when despair clutches at your ankles and every sure path seems lost in the haze, it may be time to "take this one to God." As distant as God seems at such moments, you know that you are only temporarily blinded. As soon as the fog and clouds lift, the Matterhorn will reappear; God will be there, as God always is. In the meanwhile, you can take it on faith.

50

Help God catch up on your life. Take a comfortable seat and speak your mind. You can do it quietly in your heart or out loud.

Sometimes just listening to the words you are speaking makes a difference.

51

Look up when things are looking down. Seek out the high points in the landscape of your life—whether they are skyscrapers or mountains, grandchildren or companions. Although there may be times when you cannot see them physically, you know they are with you at all times. Thank God for the landmarks that bring meaning to our lives.

52

No matter how deep your depression, no matter how difficult your situation, try to remember that there is always one more resource. You can always "take this one to God."

If you have spoken to God before, you may imagine that this "simple" approach is too difficult for you. It would be sad, indeed, if you are already in despair and then you add to this the despair of being unable to share your troubles with God. Like any other skill, talking to God requires practice. If you are having trouble getting started, here are two techniques:

53

Ask yourself what most stands in your way. Sort out your reservations and try to distinguish the most troubling. Now set that part aside and decide to deal with it last. Begin with the easiest part of the process. Build on that.

For example, if the hardest part is speaking your feelings aloud, then begin by composing your thoughts and sending them inward. Later, you will find that you can begin to speak aloud. If the hardest part is believing that God is with you, then speak first to yourself. Later, you may find that you can talk things over with God. God knows the heart. The true advantage to speaking your feelings out loud is that you yourself can listen in on the conversation.

54

If you think you cannot do this at all on your own, imagine someone in your family or one of your friends who can do this easily. If there is no one like this in your circle, imagine Sister Mary or her aunt doing this. Get a clear picture of a person who converses with God in your imagination. How would they look while speaking? Would their voice be soft or loud? Would their words be clear to others listening? How would they begin the conversation? Now put yourself in their place and do it the way that they would do it. Later, you can develop your own style.

Nothing, really, can stand in your way. God is already at your side. God already knows your heart. God anticipates the words you would say. "Taking this one to God" is a release for us—it meets a human need that dwells in us all.

Finding
New
Approaches

XIII

Humor: That Other Sense

55

Thank God for your ability to find the amusing and identify the ironic in life.

There are many theories about what sets human beings apart from the rest of Creation. Perhaps it is our brainpower. Or the secret may lie in our thumbs which make grasping almost effortless. Some say it is our cunning. Some point to our self-perception. Yet above all these is one we often fail to mention when we are asked to list our senses. We immediately think of our sight, hearing, touch, our ability to smell, and our finely developed taste buds. And it seems some of us may have a kind of sixth sense of intuition or even extrasensory perception. But all of us have one more sense: a sense of humor.

Take this little joke, for example:

When Mrs. Schwartz reached heaven, she had a strange request. "Please," she said to the greeting angel, "could I ask a question to someone who is already here?"

"If the person you want is in heaven—and if the person agrees to speak with you—I think it can be arranged," the angel said. "Who would you like to question?"

"If it's not asking too much," Mrs. Schwartz said, "I would like to see the Virgin Mary."

The angel gulped. "Well, she is certainly here. But I can only promise to ask her if she would be willing to meet with you. Of course, she is a very generous soul, so perhaps she would be willing."

It was not too long before the gracious Mary came to see Mrs. Schwartz. "Welcome to heaven," she said. "I heard you wished to ask me a question."

Mrs. Schwartz gazed at the radiant beauty of Mary almost too shy to continue. Finally, she said, "Please, if it is not too much trouble, tell me how does it feel to have a son so wonderful that millions of people worship him as a god?"

The Virgin Mary nodded and said, "My dear Mrs. Schwartz, truth be told, we were hoping he would be a doctor."

Now, I have a question for you. Is this a Jewish joke? Is it a Protestant joke? Is it a Catholic joke? Is this even a religious joke? Well, it is all of these and none of these, of course. It all depends on who is listening to it and who is telling it. But it is clear that almost anyone in Western society, from you to the Pope, could tell this joke and it might still be amusing. If you change a few details—changing the Virgin Mary to Mohammed or to Buddha's mother, for instance, and maybe removing the name Schwartz—you could even tell it outside of Western society. Humor is in the magic that our minds play as we listen and try to anticipate what's coming— especially when what is coming turns out to be more or less than what we expect. And the result? Laughter.

And the result of laughter? A lightening of the spirit, an unburdening of the heart, a sense of relief that we can get outside our usual logical existence to get a handle on something entirely illogical and maybe even a little irreverent.

There is proof that God has a sense of humor, too. Else, why would God have created Mark Twain, possibly the most impish man ever to poke fun at God? Consider how Twain describes the creation of the ordinary fly:

> *The planning of the fly was an application of pure intelligence, morals not being concerned. Not one of us could have planned the fly, not one of us could have constructed him; and no one would have considered it wise to try, except under an assumed name.*

According to Twain, it was God who gave the fly its marching orders:

> *Visit all; allow no man peace till he get it in the grave; visit and afflict the hard-worked and unoffending horse, mule, ox, ass; pester the patient cow, and all the kindly animals that labor without fair reward here and perish without hope of it hereafter; spare no creature, wild or tame; but wheresoever you find one, make his life a misery, treat him as the innocent deserve, and so please Me and increase My glory Who made the fly.*

Preposterous, you say? Is this Twain just "putting God down?" Okay, it is ironic, perhaps even humorous, but isn't it terrible to speak of God by saying that God did terrible things to us? Isn't Twain saying that God has no morals, no scruples—that God is evil, cruel, and unjust? Of course, that is one way to read Twain's story about the creation of the fly.

But something else is happening here. It is downright funny to imagine that God created a creature so malevolent and despicable that we think nothing of swatting it to keep our homes from becoming unclean.

And Twain is also comical when he shows how God's plan for the world might have been improved.

The day of rest comes but once a week, and sorry I am that it does not come oftener. Man is so consti-tuted that he can stand more rest than this. I often think regretfully that it would have been so easy to have two Sundays in a week, and yet it was not so ordained. The omnipotent Creator could have made the world in three days just as easily as He made it in six, and this would have doubled the Sundays.

When Twain carries on about the number of available Sabbaths or the creation of the fly, we have to smile. It brings some of us to laughter. Deep down, we know that Twain is not criticizing God, just poking fun at the way we think about God. And that's what all good religious humor does. It's the *human* way of thinking that is always the essence of the joke. No doubt, God enjoyed reading Twain almost as much as God enjoyed creating Twain.

Go ahead and spread some laughter of your own so that God will enjoy you as much as God enjoyed creating you.

When the scientists at the super-secret government installation finally completed building the world's fastest super-computer, they argued over what question should be put to it first. Some wanted to know more about stress analysis, some offered mathematical computations that resisted all solutions, and some wanted answers to the safe disposal of nuclear waste.

While they were arguing, a janitor came forward and said, "Ask that computer if there is a God."

Everyone fell silent as the question was put to the new wonder, and the blinking of lights and the numbers crossing the screen held their rapt attention. At last, from the speakers attached to the computer, a voice uttered, "*Now* there is."

56

*J*ust laugh. Start with a giggle and let it grow. Enjoy the way it feels. Let your mind go blank and your body shake. Laugh until you feel empty just to sense the power of laughter.

57

*D*o you feel embarrassed by the prospect of laughing out loud all by yourself? No problem. The miracle of modern television is here to serve your need. At almost any time of the day, you will find some senseless comedy on one channel or another. And lo and behold, the creators of the comedy had you in mind when they embedded a laugh-track—people chuckling at just the right places to give you a cue that you should laugh then, too. Okay, take the cue and feel the cure. Laugh along from start to finish—that should be long enough to let you sense the power of laughter.

Father Murphy died. At the gates of Heaven, he was second in line. St. Peter asked the man in front of him, "What is your name and what did you accomplish in your life?"

The man said, "My name is Joseph and I was a New York City taxi driver for twenty years." St. Peter handed Joseph a silk robe and golden scepter and said, "You may enter."

He turned next to Father Murphy, asking, "What is your name, and what did you accomplish in your life?" The answer came proudly, "I am Father Peter Murphy, and I have served God faithfully for nearly seventy years." St. Peter handed Father Murphy a cotton robe and a wooden staff, saying, "You may enter."

"Well, now," said Father Murphy, "You gave that taxi driver a silk robe and a golden scepter. Why should a servant of the Lord get only a cotton robe and a wooden staff?"

St. Peter nodded. "You have to understand. Here in Heaven we work on a *performance* basis. While you preached, everyone slept. But when he drove his taxi, everyone prayed!"

58

*I*f you have tested the power of laughter on yourself, it's time to bring some joy to your family and friends. Even if you have never told a joke before, the time has come. Learn a yarn or study a story and drop in into the conversation or include it in your next e-mail. There's a reason that people say that laughter is the best medicine, and this is your chance to discover the reason. Thank God for our sense of humor.

59

While you are at it, you might consider thanking God for all the humor and lightness that others bring to you. Whoever it may be, thank the person who brings the most laughter to your life.

60

Too many people say, "I do not have the time to read." If you are among them, collections of jokes may be just the ticket for you. The nice thing about a good book of jokes is that you can pretty much pick it up and put it down whenever and for just as much time as you want. Most jokes take only a minute or two to read. Even if you read one twice—with an eye to remembering it to tell it to someone—it hardly takes any effort at all. If we could all bring just a bit more humor into the world, we might break down just a few more barriers.

Laughing—about God, about religion, and about our beliefs—is healthy. Even the most serious among us are sometimes caught up in a moment of levity. Until someone can prove otherwise, we may as well admit that among the great miracles of the universe, laughter is one of God's finest gifts to us.

The Reverend Billy Graham tells of a time early in his ministry when he was invited to preach in a small town. He had a letter to mail, so he asked a young man to direct him to the post office. The young man gave him directions and Dr. Graham thanked him, adding, "If you are coming to church this evening, you can hear me preach."

"What are you talking about?" the young man inquired.

"Tonight's sermon is on how to get to Heaven."

"I don't think I'll be coming to hear it," the young man said. "You don't even know your way to the post office."

It may be that there are times when we do not even know the way to the post office, but that does not mean that we do not know how to laugh and reach a place that is even higher.

XIV

Controlling God

*T*his is a book about getting God on your side and getting yourself on God's side. It is not about this religion or that religion, this set of beliefs or that set of beliefs. We are open here to almost any set of beliefs trusting that we can sort them out for ourselves and make up our own minds about what works and what does not work in helping us connect with our Creator.

At the same time, organized religion plays an important role in our lives, especially as it guides us along time-honored paths. By ourselves, we certainly do not have all the wisdom that we need. And it must be admitted we modern folk tend to take less time to work out the great truths than our ancestors ever did. Everything moves at a faster pace nowadays—mail is delivered instantly, photos are either developed while you wait or appear as soon as you take them, doctors phone in prescriptions, Internet shopping is quick and easy, mass media entertainment is available twenty-four hours a day, and so on. Even our rice is instant.

Many of us prefer our religion this way, too. Bring on the short sermon, the quick fellowship circle, the brief Bible lesson, the worship service that does not last too long. Give us a message that we can absorb in ten minutes a day, but don't ask us to spend a long time contemplating. Many of us even choose our place of worship with an eye to which house of God is closest to home.

In such a world, it is difficult to imagine that any organized religion could still insist that it alone has the only truth about God and God's world. However, that is the claim made by many denominations—and you may even hear it at your own church or your own synagogue. This is not to deny that whatever your religion, there is surely wisdom in it—no doubt, a great deal of wisdom. Yet every religious person could gain a great deal by learning to listen with an open heart and an open mind.

Consider the words of Black Elk, a medicine man of the Oglala Sioux. He was born in the 1860s and died in 1950. He was the second cousin of Crazy Horse and experienced tragedy firsthand as the Native American world was shattered and circumscribed. At the same time, he witnessed a century of progress in the modern world. There is loving wisdom in Black Elk's words as he calls out to the Great Spirit:

> *Grandfather, Great Spirit, once more behold me on earth and lean to hear my feeble voice. You lived first, and you are older than all need, older than all prayer. All things belong to you—the two-legged, the four-legged, the wings of the air, and all green things that live.*
>
> *You have set the powers of the four quarters of the earth to cross each other. You have made me cross the good road and road of difficulties, and where they cross, the place is holy. Day in, day out, forevermore, you are the life of things.*

> **PEACE**
> comes within the
> souls of people
> when they
> realize...
> at the center of the universe
> dwells the Great Mystery,
> and this center is everywhere,
> it is within each of us.
> ### Black Elk

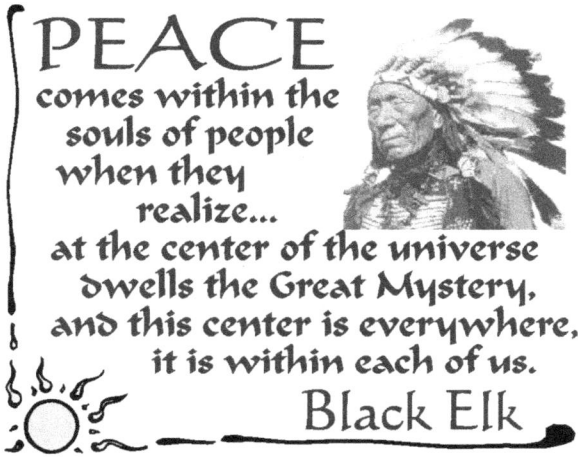

No matter what claims an organized religion makes, it must speak of God much as Black Elk does: God was first; God commands all beings; God created the world as it is, both good and evil; and God marks the places where the good and the difficult intersect as holy places. God is "the life of things."

When any religion demands obedience and exclusivity, it is attempting to control God, to limit God, to construct God in its own image. But God does not conform to the image of any single church, and the holiest of church fathers, the most reverent of preachers, the greatest of the rabbis, the wisest of the holy ones all know and all admit that God is beyond the church, beyond all human understanding.

In 1828, the Boston Missionary Society sent a missionary in upper New York State to bring the Good Word to the Iroquois. The Iroquois leader, Red Jacket, responded to the missionary with these pointed words:

> *You say that you are sent to instruct us how to worship the Great Spirit agreeably to his mind; and if we do not take hold of the religion which you white people teach, we shall be unhappy hereafter. You say that you are right and we are lost. How do*

you know this to be true? We understand that your religion is written in a book. If it was intended for us as well as for you, why has not the Great Spirit given it to us; and not only to us, but why did he not give to our forefathers the knowledge of that book, with the means of understanding it rightly? ...

If there is but one religion, why do you white people differ so much about it? Why do not all agree, as you can all read the book? ...

We also have a religion which was given to our forefathers, and has been handed down to us their children. We worship that way. It teacheth us to be thankful for all the favors we receive, to love each other, and to be united. We never quarrel about religion.

Now, if you are used to microwave popcorn and instant iced tea, if you are accustomed to lettuce that comes washed and cut and bagged so that you can effortlessly toss it in a salad bowl, and if you prefer your cream cheese whipped so it can be spread without crumbling, then it may seem natural that religion should come in a neatly wrapped package—pre-thought and predetermined. In that case, churches might be advised to put a label on the outside of the package to remind us that it contains such and such a percent, but not your full daily requirement, of spirituality.

The rest must come from within, from the place where no church has ever been; the place where preachers' words

One God * Many Paths

One God * Many Paths

reach, but only to be weighed; the place where all you have been told is mulled over and assessed; the place that only you and God inhabit, your soul. Deep in this place, you know that you and your neighbors—white, red, yellow, brown, and black—are all equally blessed by God's presence. Even how they dress on the outside—whether they wear the black garment of the Friends or the black frock of the Hasidic Jews, whether they wear the bright kanga of Africa or the deep-dyed sari of India—is only a celebration of the inner self. Between souls, there can be no prejudice; souls reach out to other souls, needing to join together because the little bit of God in each of us wishes always to be part of the God of all of us.

61

What is your skin color? To see how little it matters, take the measure of people of another color. They are around you day by day. If you are black, seize an extra moment to speak to the white waitress at the restaurant. Does she have children? Is she happy with her job or does she have ambitions for something else? If you are white, find a moment to talk with a black person. If you can, strike up a conversation with an Inuit or a Native American. Thank God for the diversity that makes us so intriguing to one another.

62

What is your church? Make a deal with a friend to go once to his or her church and invite her or him to come once to yours. Ask a priest about Catholicism, talk to a Methodist minister, have a conversation with a rabbi. Don't be afraid. Their object is not to convince you that your church is not right for you, only that other churches and synagogues are also on the spiritual path. Whatever you take away from your experience will enrich your personal quest.

63

Strike a blow against prejudice. Don't be afraid of your neighbor. Remember Sourpuss Smithers, that character from Frank Capra's classic film, *Meet John Doe*? Smithers' neighbors shunned him for years believing that he was unfriendly. Even when they said hello in passing, Sourpuss never answered. But it turned out that he was not an angry old man; he was just hard of hearing. When they learned the truth about him, they discovered he was as good a fellow as the next and a very friendly neighbor, indeed. You may think that a Jew or Puerto Rican or Black or Guatemalan or Catholic or Baptist or whatever who lives down the way is unfriendly or mean-spirited or even dangerous. However, after a moment or two of conversation, you may find that he or she is much like you—wants the same things for his or her children that you want for yours, thinks about the same kind of God that you think about, feels the same way about politicians and morticians as you do, and more. Thank God for the times when people share their souls instead of hiding them.

To be ourselves fully and openly, we need to stop trying to control God and start letting God control us.

XV

Walkabout

Most of us spend a great deal of time working. We *have* bosses, or we *are* bosses, and sometimes we are even caught between bosses. Many of us have to record the hours we work, accounting for our whereabouts five or six days out of every week. Even those who are highly skilled specialists— doctors, lawyers, surgeons, therapists, programmers, consultants, and the like—have only their time to sell, and that means keeping zealous logs of hours and sometimes even of minutes. And despite all the time-saving conveniences of modern life, even keeping a household up and running requires constant effort. This means more work after normal work hours: cooking meals, cleaning up, paying bills, filing taxes, and maintaining contact with distant family through phone calls and correspondence.

From time to time, though, a person comes up for air and asks, "What about me?" The answer is different for each of us. It could be that this is the moment we choose to start a new regimen such as running or walking. It could be that this is the moment we decide to join a local gymnasium. It could be that this is the moment we decide to take a vacation. It could be that this is the moment we go out to buy new makeup or new clothing. Or it could just be a moment when we reach for chocolate. Any or all of these, in our society, can be considered a life change.

But what if the question persists? What if you are haunted by it? "What about me?" Then you may decide that you are missing something very important. Your true Self is absent; it is missing in action. You go about your daily life, but it seems almost meaningless. It is difficult to share this feeling with others. They somehow seem to be so well-adjusted (or, at the least, adjusted)—it is only you that seems to be out of kilter. And if it is your true Self that you have lost, it is almost certain that no one else can find it for you.

Even if you continue functioning on the outside, you know on the inside that you have reached a crisis. But you would be wrong to blame this on our society, on the way we drive ourselves to keep busy. Actually, you have reached a crisis that has been common in almost all societies since the beginning of time. Early Christians took themselves off to the desert or to caves to become hermits while looking for their spiritual selves. They were following the model of Jesus who had been led out into the wilderness for forty days and forty nights to confront Satan. And Jesus may have been following the model of the Children of Israel who had wandered for forty years in the wilderness as God waited for their true selves to emerge.

Other societies have developed rituals or customs to help people in spiritual crises. Shamans guide individuals on spiritual journeys, and Medicine Men exorcize demons to make a person whole again, but among all the peoples of the earth, one of the most unique answers comes from the world of the Australian Aborigines. This is "walkabout."

When an Aborigine faces the "What about me?" crisis, she or he knows precisely what to do. If the true Self is lost, then it is imperative that it be found. Everything else is put on hold. The Aborigine just says, "I'm going walkabout."

Leaving all possessions behind, taking only what is absolutely necessary, the Aborigine seeker walks away from the group. In theory, the journey continues until you meet your true Self. If you happen to encounter other people before you find your true Self, you don't avoid them as they may be part of your destiny, or they may be there because you *need* to encounter them. If you happen to chance upon animals, you study them to see if they answer any of your spiritual needs. If you happen to come upon a particular place, you study whether this place has special meaning for you. In other words, walkabout is a search without definition. It assumes that if you chance upon your true Self, you will recognize it.

When you find your Self, the Aborigines believe, it should be an occasion for a conversation. You should talk with your Self, stating what the walkabout has taught you. You should tell your Self all that can be told. But you should be conscious of the fact that some things are beyond words—your feelings, your intuition, the spirit of your meeting. In a sense, when you are finished, you are ready to return as a whole person, a complete individual, a healed soul.

For us, walkabout is as much a symbol as a reality. It is very different from a vacation. By definition, it is not the kind of thing that people can do together. You are on your own. Maybe that is why it is so difficult to share this kind of personal crisis with other people in the first place. You need a space, a place, a time to find your true Self. You cannot hire a guide as you would to climb a mountain. You can only be guided by what happens when you set out, what you encounter along the way, and what you have learned when you face your Self again.

There are no real rules. Every walkabout will be unique. But here are some ideas for getting you started. If you are among the many who are asking, "What about me?" you might consider some of the following:

64

Make a reservation for one. Choose the kind of landscape that you feel will challenge you. If you are a city person, try a camp site or a lodge in a national or state park. If you are a small-town type, consider a motel in the heart of a big city.

65

Don't plan your journey as you would if you were a tourist. Don't take a camera. The images on your walkabout will be best taken through your own eyes and in your own memory. Don't follow a map. Feel free to wander, to encounter, to find new feelings in new places.

64

If you encounter a new person who seems significant, do not be afraid to relate to that person. It might be someone hiking the same trail you are hiking or someone staring at the same painting in the museum that attracts you. If you find a site that feels "right" to you, spend some time there looking for your true Self. It could be a forest grove or a university campus. If there is a good feeling, stay with it.

65

For most of us, walkabout cannot last indefinitely. Most of us need to continue our work and return to our families, either to take care of those who rely on us or to maintain our livelihood. If your first walkabout does not end in a complete success, don't fight it. Try it again some other time. You may find that just the act of "going walkabout," as they say in Australia, will be enough to refresh you.

66

If you have a family, a spouse, a partner, or a significant other, remember that they need reassurance. Let them know beforehand that your going off alone is not a way of avoiding being with them—just as it is important for you to know that there may come a time when they may decide to "go walkabout," too.

If you think about the models of Jesus and the Children of Israel, you will realize this is a religious quest, a spiritual journey. To be God-like, each of us must first be wholehearted. We should seek unity in our selves just as we believe that God models unity in the universe. Going walkabout may help.

XVI

Reclaiming Your Life

> The weak can never forgive.
> Forgiveness is the attribute of the strong.
> *Mahatma Gandhi*

There is a whole mess of "ness" words in our pop vocabulary. The following pop to mind: "wholeness," "willingness," "wellness," "centeredness," "creativeness," "happiness," "consciousness," "cleanliness" (right next to "Godliness"), and "kindness." Advice columns are filled with "ness" words every day. But even the writers of advice columns don't always go all the way.

Take Ann Landers and Dear Abby, for example. Believe it or not, these two competitive ladies were twin sisters born seventeen minutes apart. Ann Landers was born Esther Pauline Friedman. Abigail Van Buren ("Dear Abby") was born Pauline Esther Friedman. A few months after Esther began writing her advice column as Ann Landers, her twin sister began writing the Dear Abby column.

The sisters were obviously competitive. Word soon got around that Pauline had offered her Dear Abby column at a reduced rate to their hometown newspaper in Sioux City provided that the *Sioux City Journal* would agree not to carry the Ann Landers column. That was in 1956. In 1958, the feud between the sisters was made public by *Life* magazine. In 1964, the sisters announced that they had "made up." In truth, the competition between them was too stiff and the rift too deep. They never reconciled. Even after Ann Landers (Esther) died in 2002, her daughter (who writes the "Dear Prudence" column) was still arguing with the daughter of Pauline (who had taken over the "Dear Abby" column). Imagine! These extraordinary women who gave (and give) sound advice to millions of people could not bury the hatchet and share the spotlight!

The missing "ness" was "forgive*ness*." It is probably the hardest "ness" in the human vocabulary. This may be why Christianity understands the forgiveness of our sins as the mission of Jesus, and why Judaism sets aside a day of fasting each year to secure God's forgiveness. Both Christianity and Judaism rely on God's forgiveness even while reminding us that we must not confuse this with our need to reconcile with one another. As Robert Ingersoll once put it, "If I owe Smith ten dollars, and God forgives me, that doesn't pay Smith."

Forgiving other human beings is not easy. It is far more popular to harbor hatred or jealousy or enmity as visitors in the heart. Over time, these inner visitors become more and more a part of us. We hardly recognize ourselves in the mirror without their presence written all over our faces. Getting them out, exorcizing them, ridding ourselves of long-held feuds is not work for the weak; it requires diligent effort. So the question is, "What do I get in return for all that work?"

The answer is health, particularly mental health. Hatred in the heart befogs the mind and shuts out light. If a falling

out with a relative, friend, acquaintance, or co-worker has festered for a long time, you already know the truth of this. Far from being able to put that person out of your mind, his or her image haunts you. Thoughts of vengeance, petty or violent, linger in the imagination. Memories of how you believe you were wronged disturb you. Feelings of ill-will can become obsessive. In the end, you find yourself *needing* the hatred, *needing* your enemy in order to know yourself. You may even arrive at the poet Heinrich Heine's conclusion: "One should forgive one's enemies but not before they are hanged." Before you get there, stop, think, and rethink.

God can help; forgiveness is a divine attribute. Human beings need forgiveness precisely because we are *not* perfect. We need to forgive one another for the same reason. Without forgiving others, and without being forgiven by them, we could never experience love—God's love *or* human love.

69

Put some time each day into the *art* of forgiving. Just think of someone who has done you wrong and begin to imagine ways you might choose to forgive that wrong. Thank God for forbearance.

70

Ask someone who has been avoiding you, or someone who thinks you have hurt him or her in some way, to forgive you. It doesn't matter whether you think that you have actually done wrong. If you are strong enough, you can be the one to ask forgiveness.

71

Cast out the demon and have a housecleaning of the heart! Make the first move by forgiving someone you think has hurt you. Of course, this means being in contact with a person you have been avoiding. This may seem too sudden. You may wish to start with a greeting card, a small gift, or a token. Follow your instinct. Sudden forgiveness can be jarring. Making gentle moves toward forgiveness can be healing.

When it comes to forgiveness, you need not look outside yourself. You were created with all the inner strength you need, but ill-will or antipathy may hide your strength and convince you that you are weak. When you feel your strength again, you will know that the real you is back!

72

*D*eclare victory. When you forgive someone or when someone forgives you, celebrate it! Make it an occasion. Break out a bottle of something you have been saving. Have a gathering and offer a toast. Dance. Sing. Thank God for restoring your soul.

Declare VICTORY For Your Heart's Sake

XVII

Say It with Powers

Little Michael was alone in the backyard playing. He had his mother's broom for a horse, and he was galloping through steep canyons in his imagination. Now and again, he would stop and shoot out his index finger at some imaginary outlaw hiding in the bushes. As the sky darkened, Michael tired of his game and went back into the house to watch television.

A while later, his mother's voice came from the kitchen. "Mikey, have you seen the broom?"

"I think I left it outside, Mom," Michael called back.

His mother appeared and stood between Michael and the television. "Would you please go out and get it for me?"

Michael looked up sheepishly. "It's dark outside. Do I have to go out there alone?"

"You know there's nothing to worry about," his mother said. "You are never really alone. God is out there, too."

So little Michael went to the back door and opened it a crack. He peeked out and whispered, "God, since you are already out there, please hand me the broom."

Prayer is always intended for a purpose. Many prayers are requests: for healing, for wealth, for a safe journey, for help finding a misplaced broom. It only stands to reason that if God is our parent, and God is all powerful, God should be able to help us with our creaturely needs. It also stands to reason that God is not required to answer every such prayer. Like any parent, God can say, "No."

There are other types of prayer, too. If we say grace before meals, we are thanking God for the food that is before us. We know that the chicken came plucked and cut up and packaged in shrink-wrap. We know it was purchased at a local grocery with cash that we earned. And we know that the chicken was sold to the grocery by a wholesaler who bought it from a chicken farmer. And we know that the chicken farmer raised the chicken using grain that he had to purchase. And so on. But we are acknowledging the fact that be-

He
prayeth well, who loveth well
Both man and bird and beast.
He prayeth best, who loveth best
All things both great and small;
For the dear God who loveth us
He made and loveth all.
Samuel Taylor Coleridge

yond all these mundane actions, the chicken on our table is a result of the miracle of Creation, the design of a universe that allows for there to be a cycle of life and death, a cycle of rainy and dry seasons, a cycle of growth and harvest, an orderly existence. We know that without these, all our work would be in vain. Indeed, if any of these were interrupted, we and our families would face starvation and death. When we thank God, then, we are not only expressing our gratitude for what is presently before us, we are also reminding ourselves of our continuing need for God's grace. In the end, we are not eating at *our* table, we are always eating at *God's* table.

There is thus a delicate and subtle balance between the farmer's simple prayer for rain in its season and our prayer of thanks for food. We can sense it readily when it comes to sustenance; it is a little less simple to glimpse when we thank God for a glorious sunset, a charming rainbow, or an elegant orchid. Even these prayers, however, remind us of the need for God's continuing cycle of grace since our prayer is never just for *this* sunset but for *this* sunset among *all* sunsets. So every prayer of thanks is also a prayer expressing our continuing needs. A grateful prayer thanking God for the gift of a child at the instant of birth also implies a thousand prayers asking for God's help with every aspect of that child's life from that moment forward.

Children often intuitively sense the connection between asking and thanking. They hear it in adult prayers because their ears are fresh and new and because to them the words have to make sense in their world. Take the little girl who prayed, "And forgive us our trash baskets as we forgive those who put trash in our baskets." Or the little boy who ended his prayer with, "Lead us not into temptation, but deliver us some e-mail. Amen." Their simple mistakes point to the need for us to pray about things that matter to us.

But prayer does not come naturally to many of us. Just sensing beauty around us does not always translate into

prayer. Just knowing that our daily work is blessed does not translate into thanking God for a job that we may both love and hate at the same time. One preacher compared this to flying a kite. There are times when you get the tail of the kite just right, when the wind seems just right, when the kite seems just right, and yet, run as you might, the kite just refuses to fly. Other times, the kite just lifts off the ground and takes to the air with ease. Some of it is luck, but a lot of it is just practice. A lot of success in prayer is practice, too.

73

When you are ready to practice prayer, take into account the five "P"s for getting started: 1) Find a good *place* for prayer, a comfortable place for you. 2) Practice praying in the same *period* of time each day until you feel accustomed to praying anytime. 3) Find a comfortable *posture* for prayer. Decide whether you prefer standing or sitting, kneeling or lying down. 4) Start with a *passage* from Scripture or from poetry or from your prayer book. 5) And now that the kite seems right, and the tail seems right, and the wind seems right, *pray*.

All this is fine for getting started, but the success of prayer is still a matter for the heart. And the heart is not attuned to finding God in the same *place* and the same *period* of time every day. The heart does not respond only in a particular *posture* or to any particular *passage*, no matter how you choose it. It is the *presence* of God that is the sixth "P." And prayer is most apt to be heartfelt and sincere when we sense that *presence*.

Prayer practice only prepares us for the real thing. When we truly need forgiveness, that is the best time to ask for forgiveness. When we truly need healing, that is the best time to ask for healing. When our daily bread is truly before us, that is the best time to thank God for our food. This is a case where examples speak louder than prescriptions. Here are a dozen heartfelt prayers that can help us find our own right times:

74

*T*hank God for a loving spouse, for loving siblings, for loving parents, for a loving family, and for loving friends.

75

*T*hank God for your spiritual family—for those you interact with online and for those you interact with in person.

76

Thank God for the night when you can sleep and be refreshed. Thank God for the morning that returns you to the living.

77

Ask God to use you to work toward the Kingdom of God—to guide you to be a good example of a Christian, a good example of a Muslim, a good example of a Hindu, a good example of a Jew.

78

Thank God for helping you know that with God present, nothing is impossible.

79

Ask God to bring joy into your soul, pleasure into your heart, skill into your hands, music into your ears, beauty into your eyes, purpose into your steps, and wisdom into your ways.

80

Thank God for your human capacity to learn great things from little things and little things from great things.

81

Thank God for the seasons—for the spring that renews life, for the summer that shows us the meaning of growth, for the fall that brings glorious harvest and stunning color, and for the winter that reveals the meaning of rest and of death.

82

And thank God for the seasons of our lives—for infancy and its unbounded potential, for childhood and its talent for play and joy, for adolescence and its gift for love and for its abounding gift for mixing learning and naivete, for adulthood with its ambitions and its opportunities for us to

make the most of ourselves, for parenthood along with its ability to remind us of all that has come before it, for maturity that helps us learn satisfaction in what we have actually achieved, and for old age with its wisdom of the ways of the world and for its chance to reward others with all that we have gained.

83

Ask God to give you the chance to be God's hands in the world—to help those in need, to give of your gifts to those who need gifts, to make music for others, to join in our dances of joy, and to share with those who need sympathy and healing.

84

Thank God for the quiet times—times when you can sense God's presence in the wonders of simplicity.

85

Thank God for the tumultuous times that make God's presence known to us all, that force us to reach out to one another, that make us aware of our mission to bring order out of chaos, and that give us so many opportunities to do just that.

And, above all,

86

Thank God for the moments of peace—for the good times that remind us that God's ultimate peace can be realized here on earth as it is above. For it is in times of peace that we can turn our full attention to helping one another, to being present for one another, to bringing the meaning of God's love to one another, to being most like God ourselves.

Herein is the most powerful meaning of prayer—that it speaks to us as much as it speaks to God, and that through prayer, we learn what we need most and how to achieve it. And too, that prayer is our way of speaking, aloud or in a whisper, the dreams that we have for ourselves and the visions that we have for one another. Every prayer is more an answer than a question.

XVIII

Separations

A recent study analyzed the top ten reasons behind divorce in the United States. Reasons nine and ten came in at a dead heat, with as many people claiming "boredom" as those who claimed that they "fell in love with another person." "Physical abuse" was reason number eight, pointing to an age-old malaise that puts our whole society to shame. The seventh main reason for divorce—"spouse did not make enough money"— is well-known to us all, as is the sixth reason, "unsatisfactory sex."

The fifth main reason given for divorce was "falling out of love." One woman added the comment, "I was unsure if I still loved my spouse. That told me I didn't. I was brave enough to leave the marriage." The fourth reason was "emotional abuse" and the third was "constant fighting." There were remarks like, "We fought nonstop during my first year of marriage" and "What did we do most of the time? We fought, fought, fought."

Not surprisingly, the second most-cited reason for divorce was "infidelity." The only possible surprise was that this answer was almost equally common among men as it was among women. This may indicate that though infidelity is a cause, it may also be a symptom of additional marital problems. Husbands and wives may stray, not because they have a wayward nature, but because they are suffering from other problems on the list.

This brings us to the number one reason for divorce in the United States: "communication problems." Some women remarked, "He doesn't understand who I am." Some men replied, "She doesn't know me." One woman said, "My husband was a hundred percent inattentive and thought only of himself." One man noted, "My wife and I were not communicating."

Divorce is not the only separation we face in life. When loved ones die, the living are left behind. When grown children go off to college or join the armed forces, parents face empty nests, and the young feel temporarily disoriented. When new jobs are in distant cities, families and friends may be torn apart leaving important people behind and causing those who move away all the dislocation of relocation. Separation is a fact of life and always has been. All separations have at least this one thing in common: the loss of communication.

The same study that polled the ten top reasons for divorce also asked for the main reasons for marriage in the first place. Here, a majority answered "love." Ranking just below love was "need for companionship" and "fear of growing old alone." Just like separation, our needs for love, warmth, and companionship are facts of life. It's no wonder the words "community" and "communication" come from the same root!

In the Bible, when Jacob was forced to separate from his family ("community"), he dreamed of a ladder or stairway connecting Heaven and earth ("communication"). In the dream, God promised to be with Jacob in all his travels. In our own lives, when separations are forced upon us, we can fall back on that ladder and that promise. No two places can be far distant when earth and Heaven are so closely connected. God is here with us, but God is also with those far away from us.

This thought that everything is connected and communication is always possible is soothing to many who are separated from loved ones. However, it may be less than soothing to those couples whose divorce is bitter or, to those families whose children have become the apparent victims. And yet even in these all-too-familiar circumstances, there can be some relief in knowing that the children of divorce also have God for protection and company, and a former spouse may often feel bound to overcome vengeful feelings and ill-will to act in God-like ways.

For all of us caught in the eternal rise and fall of meeting and separation, the knowledge that God connects all relationships can be a source of healing. We can make new friends or even re-establish family ties, but we are never forced to relinquish old feelings or abandon those we have left or those who have left

us. The definition of "home" may change, but "going home" is always possible.

87

The Internet makes it easy to search for old friends, for former classmates, for people we have not seen for years. There are even professional services to do the searching for you. There are questions, though: What will you do when you find someone you thought you lost? Can you just strike up a conversation as if the years never intervened? Will you still have much in common with him or her? It takes some courage to make the search. It takes more courage to make the contact. To put it bluntly, being alone can sometimes be the result of cowardice. It is only when you stiffen your resolve to make contact that you realize how much strength God has given you.

We all know that separations cause us to go through stages of adjustment. There are turning points and signals: There is grief. There is loneliness. There is a sense of loss. There is healing. There is readjustment. Along the way, some people lose themselves in one stage or another while others proceed from step to step. Denial happens, as does sudden creativity. Some people try for "normalcy" too quickly. Some find it difficult to ever feel "normal" again. Many people find therapy helpful. Others find help in the church or synagogue, in teachings and ministers, in yoga and meditation, and in the spiritual community.

88

The connection between Heaven and earth can help. When you feel stuck at some stage, unable to resume your life without help, the time has come to send a prayer. On Jacob's ladder, the angels traveled up and then down. We, too, know that we can only expect answers to messages that we actually send. In the many forms of twelve-step therapy, the first step is admitting that there is a problem. The second step is believing that a Power greater than ourselves can help us. In sending our prayers upward for Heaven's help, we take these two steps up the ladder.

89

File your petition with God. At moments of separation, we may find many reasons to deny God, or we may vilify God, or we may complain to God. All of these are valid responses. You are not the only one who has ever felt this way. Betrayal was one of the emotions felt by the Apostles when Jesus was crucified. Go ahead and complain to God. God designed us, and it was God who built the suffering of separation in us. At the same time, God gave us independent minds and freedom of choice so that we could challenge God. There is no reason that we should not exercise that freedom. Honesty demands it. And, God knows, exercising this option may bring some relief.

It helps to remember the connection between "community" and "communication." It is not just with the people who are near us that we develop relationships. Lasting friendships have been known to blossom among people who have never met face-to-face. Family ties have become strong between members of families who live at great distances from one another. Separation does not put an end to communication; it only changes the means of communication. Separation does not end community; it only broadens the meaning of community.

90

Make your own "community scrapbook." Collect all those old photos of friends and family who are part of your greater community. Tell those you miss to send you more photos for your album. Take photos when relatives visit. Make your scrapbook more vivid by "journaling"—giving pages titles and writing memories or short paragraphs on each page. Put in a page for God (you can use photographs of nature or you can just leave a space where the photograph should obviously have been). Next time you feel alone, pull out your community scrapbook and experience the warmth around you. The way God made us, separation is only a state of mind.

XIX

God's Gift

> All that we see
> or seem,
> is but a dream
> within a dream.
> *Edgar Allan Poe*

When we have difficulty solving a problem, we sometimes offer to "sleep on it." When we need to be creative, we
may try to "dream something up." When we hear an improbable proposal, we often call it an "idle dream." When our attention is distracted and we stare out into space, we may
catch ourselves "daydreaming." And when we speak of our
highest aspirations, our ultimate goals in life, we often call
them "dreams."

We are constantly and nonchalantly swapping dreams
with family or friends in casual conversation. At times, this
produces new interpretations or raises highly pertinent
questions that result in an outpouring of similar dreams.
Sometimes listeners are polite but dismiss our dream as if it

had not been told or had not been heard. And some people claim that they never dream or say that they never remember their dreams.

91

Everyone dreams whether or not their dreams are remembered. According to dream researchers, if you have trouble remembering your dreams, you can increase your odds in a few simple ways. First, fall asleep telling yourself to remember what you dream. Second, as soon as you wake up, lie still for five minutes or so in the position you were in before you turned off your alarm clock and try to recall your dream. Third, as soon as you recall it, write down as much as you can remember of it. Last, it often happens that a dream we had at night comes back at an odd moment during the day. When this occurs, you should immediately jot down what you remember of the dream.

Why do we tend to share our dreams mainly in casual conversation? After all, dreaming is an essential part of our lives, an inner natural resource. Dreams are experiences just as waking events are experiences. Nearly all of us ask one another for help with events that occur in our family lives, in the workplace, and in society at large. Then why do we tend to slip our dreams into our conversations almost as an afterthought?

"What a dream! The princess was trapped and the dragon just kept on belching fire..."

One reason, of course, is that dreams do not fit comfortably into our everyday lives, and visions (*day* dreams) are even less likely to be considered "normal." For instance, if a co-worker spent the first part of every morning sharing dreams with office mates, he or she would not last long on the job. The job is important and essential; by comparison, dreams and visions are thought frivolous at best, and at worst they are considered indicators of neuroses and psychoses. These are societal "norms."

Nevertheless, dreams are "an-*other*" world for us. In the laboratory, scientists can tell *when* we are dreaming by watching various physical signs (things like eye movement, muscle relaxation, and brain wave activity), but they cannot tell us *what* we are dreaming or what our dreams mean. Therapists and spiritual guides can help us to interpret our dreams, but these interpretations are only "valid" if we ourselves agree they are—and even then our every dream can be interpreted again and again, revealing many new and different truths.

No scientist and no therapist can tell us *why* dreaming is a part of human nature or *where* our dreams come from. Sometimes, we suspect we know. It doesn't take a rocket scientist to recognize that a large helping of pizza with pepperoni and anchovies can make for telltale dreams. And it doesn't take a Ph.D. to explain that nightmares visit us in times of stress. But explanations like these only account for a handful of our dreams in a whole lifetime of dreaming.

By contrast, there is infinite potential for mystery and wonder in the third of our lives that we spend sleeping. From ancient times to today, dreams have been delivering messages to us from some place deep inside of us—or, perhaps, from some place far outside of us. Nearly every civilization has believed—and nearly every religion has taught at one time or another—that some of our dreams are direct communications from God. Even if we are skeptical, if we think that our dreams come from deep inside us, there is still the unavoidable truth that the "us" who is dreaming was created by God to receive the dream.

Treat Yourself
to a Dream

92

Throughout human history there has been a tradition of purposely "incubating" dreams. Incubating means "planting the seed" to receive a dream message simply by asking God to send you a dream. You may be surprised if you try this. If you keep asking night after night, chances are you will soon receive not only a dream, but a memorable dream.

If you have been granted a memorable dream, particularly if you receive the same dream more than once, you have still only begun the process. As one first-century sage stated: "A dream that is not interpreted is like a letter that has gone unread." And most of us have a lot of "d-mail" (dream mail) that goes unopened.

The interpretation of a few dream messages is simple. If you dream that you are unhappy at work, it might *just* mean that you are unhappy at work. If you dream of flying away, it might *just* mean that you need a vacation. But dream messages are seldom that clear. Dreams come to us in images and colors and feelings. Because they are connected to our deepest creativity, they wear disguises and present us with dramas that do not always make immediate sense.

Nor do books explaining dreams always hold the answer. These books, filled with notes on the various symbols in our dreams along with statements about what the symbols mean, are part of a long tradition. Dream dictionaries like these go back to papyrus scrolls found in Egypt and clay tablets unearthed in Mesopotamia. The definitions you read today are not much different from the ones written in ancient times. Lists of dream symbols are okay as far as they go, but they really don't go all that far. Just knowing that once upon a time, "dreaming of riding on an ox" meant "you will rise to greatness" may make you feel like you know what to expect, but how many people nowadays dream of riding on an ox? Rocket ships in dreams may be phallic symbols, or they may tell you that you are thinking about making a long journey, but if you work for Harley-Davidson or General Electric or

NASA, for example, then they may well have another and a somewhat more important meaning for you.

93

*D*reams are always personal. If you want to know what your dreams mean, you have to think about what they mean to *you*, within the context of *your* world and *your* life. You also have to share them with people who know you, people who can think about what they might mean to you from a point-of-view outside your own. Generally, every character in your dream is actually you, or a part of you, even if the characters are masquerading as friends, family, or strangers. When you have an idea of what your dream is about, or when you hear an interpretation that makes sense, you begin to get the dream's message—at least, one of its possible messages.

In dreams, no one comes between you and God. What is deepest in your heart is fully exposed, even all the things you hide during the day. You don't have to worry about not being accustomed to prayer, about being shy at thanking God in public, about not being perfect in some way. Dreams bring us guidance, help us through difficult moments, inspire healing, and serve as comforting companions in times of transition. How you use your dreams is up to you, but why not consider using them to get in touch with the Divine within you?

94

Ask God for guidance in your dreams. Are you having trouble with a teenage son or daughter? Have you lost a job? Are you wondering whether to make a commitment to a new person? Do you feel lost in a swamp of smothering difficulties? Sleep on it. Shape a question for God and hold that question in your mind—setting aside the problem itself—as you relax to fall asleep. Just as in asking for God to send you a message, this technique of incubating a dream by asking God to answer a specific question often bears fruit.

95

Choose a dream. Imagine the scene. Imagine the characters. Imagine the place. Imagine the topic that your dream folk should discuss or the actions they should take. See what develops. Many find it simple to control the content of dreams; others find it more difficult. But when it happens—either naturally or through practice—you discover a whole new world of experiences. And when you wake, you will probably be ready to thank God for the incredible gift of dreaming.

96

Or ask for a dream gift. Join people like Albert Einstein, Anaïs Nin, Paul McCartney, Virginia Woolf, Ingmar Bergman, George Frederick Handel, Richard Wagner, Robert Louis Stevenson, Eleanor Roosevelt, Billy Joel, Charlotte and Emily Brontë, Samuel Taylor Coleridge, Carl Jung, Orson Welles, Mary Shelly, D. H. Lawrence, Sigmund Freud, and Jack Nicklaus. Every one of them—and countless thousands of others—all received special gifts in their dreams. If you come out of your own dream with a gift—whether it is the inspiration for a poem, a song, a personal mantra, an insight, a new strength, a new career, or a delicious recipe for chicken—you will probably be ready to thank God for the gifts that dreams may bring.

97

Have you ever awakened from a dream into half-sleep and thought to yourself, "That was a wonderful dream," and closed your eyes and decided to go back into the same dream? If so, you were taking the first step into "lucid dreaming." In lucid dreaming, you take control over your dream world. You decide what you will do in your dream, even while you are dreaming. If this seems strange to you, consider how strange the dream world itself is. On the one hand, it is entirely outside of our waking experience. On the other hand, it is just as genuine as our waking world. As the Chinese sage Chuang-tzu once said on awakening, "I do not know whether I was then a man dreaming I was a butterfly, or whether I am now a butterfly dreaming I am a man." We can all thank God for giving us the rich and magical world of our dreams.

> A dream that is not interpreted is like a letter that has gone unread.

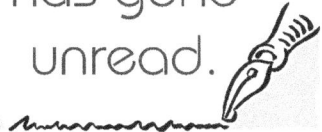

Most magnificent of all is the chance we have to share dreams with one another, to paint our images in the minds of family and friends, and to see the paintings of their dream images in our minds. The dream world is a rich and vibrant source for sharing.

98

Make time for dream-sharing. The best time may be at the breakfast table when your dreams are still fresh in your mind. Or if you write your dreams down upon awakening, you can choose to share them later. The important thing is to make a set time to share your dreams. And not just your dreams; it is also the perfect time for sharing your hopes, aspirations, and life goals.

99

Most intriguing of all is the opportunity to "plant a dream," for example, as you put your child to sleep at night. For many years, my twins and I decided *where* we would meet in our dreams. Some of our favorite places were "near the pond beside the castle wall," "in the courtyard of the princess," and "in the shade of the Tree of Life." My twin daughters are full-grown now, but they still recall our dream "meetings" vividly. Thank God for that most exceptional of all human gifts—the gift of imagination.

Because the world of dreams is so accessible to us all, and because it is a wealth of resources we all possess, and because it can be used in so many ways to put us in touch both with the God who is our Creator and the part of God we harbor deep inside ourselves, I saved the subject of dreams to the very end of our time together. In dreams, God is *always* on your side.

In a profound metaphor, every prayer is a dream we speak. Every time we thank God; every time we do something to help our neighbors because it helps us bring more of God into our world; every time we do something to make ourselves feel better or to bring a little joy to other folk; every time we remember the blessings we have and recall that our shortcomings and our illnesses are opportunities for us to stretch and to learn; every time we celebrate instead of complaining; every time we seek help instead of sinking deeper into a personal mire; every time we hear the symphony of life and know that all its movements ebb and flow and that its themes require balance—beginning, middle, and end—to be truly beautiful; every time we notice the great things and feel small; every time we notice the small things and feel great—we take part in a human dream that never ends.

This little book contains 100 ways that we can find God within us, help others to see God in action, find answers to questions we ask, and be challenged by God to be more than even we think we can be. Every way is a way to get God on our side or for us to get on God's side. The 100th way was the one that started me on the path to writing this book. If even one of the many suggestions has been helpful to you or resonates in your heart, I think you will understand when I say:

100

Thank God for giving us this chance to talk. Thank God for allowing us these moments together. Thank God for the possibility, the very nearly mystical possibility, for people—even people who have never seen one another face to face—to make a difference in one another's lives. As for me, I thank God for *you.*

About the Author

Seymour Rossel is a publisher, teacher, rabbi, and educator. He is the author of more than thirty books and editor of several hundred.

Seymour studied at the Jerusalem Institute for Youth Leaders, Southern Methodist University, and New York University. For many years, he served the Jewish Reform movement as national Director of the Department of Education, as publisher of the national UAHC press, as Dean of the School of Education of Hebrew Union College-Jewish Institute of Religion in New York, and as Director of the Joint Commission on Jewish Education. He was Executive Vice-President of Behrman House, Inc., a Jewish publishing firm specializing in textbooks and curriculum. And he is currently President of Rossel Counseling and Consulting and Publisher at Rossel Books.

For many years he has enjoyed teaching elective courses in Bible, archaeology, and spirituality at the Women's Institute of Houston. Presenting lectures, workshops, and retreats on connecting with God, modern spirituality, Bible, and dreams for Jewish and Christian groups, he has traveled extensively throughout North America, Great Britain, and Israel. A fuller biography is available at Wikipedia and more information on his speaking tours and availability may be found at *https://RosselBooks.com.*

www.ingramcontent.com/pod-product-compliance
Lightning Source LLC
Chambersburg PA
CBHW022010090426
42741CB00007B/964